on nurturing christians * *

on nurturing christians

perhaps a manifesto for education

wayne r. rood

ABINGDON PRESS
NASHVILLE NEW YORK

ON NURTURING CHRISTIANS

Copyright © 1972 by Abingdon Press

All rights in this book are reserved. No part of the book may be reproduced in any manner whatsoever without written permission of the publishers except brief quotations embodied in critical articles or reviews. For information address Abingdon Press, Nashville, Tennessee.

ISBN 0-687-28883-5

Library of Congress Catalog Card Number: 74-186831

Lines from "The Answer" by Robinson Jeffers, from *The Selected Poetry of Robinson Jeffers*, copyright 1937, by Robinson Jeffers, are used by permission of Random House, Inc.

The quotation from *East of Eden* by John Steinbeck, copyright 1952 by John Steinbeck, is reprinted by permission of The Viking Press, Inc.

MANUFACTURED BY THE PARTHENON PRESS AT NASHVILLE, TENNESSEE, UNITED STATES OF AMERICA

CONTENTS

PROLOGUE 7

I. SCHOOLING 13
   1. The Logic Breakthrough 16
   2. The Knowledge Explosion 22
   3. The Communication Marvel 26
   4. The School Revolt 30
   5. Alternative Schooling 40
   6. A Stirring of Spirit 47

INTERLOGUE 53
   1. Christian Education 53
   2. Christian Teaching 60

ON NURTURING CHRISTIANS

II. NURTURING 69
   1. Source 69
   2. Scene 95
   3. Stance 119
   4. Style 145

EPILOGUE 165

BIBLIOGRAPHY 171

PROLOGUE ✣ ✣

Christians are a nurturing people.

They know from their own religious experience that it is a growing thing. With some the beginning is not even noticeable, with others the start is dramatic. Thereafter it turns out to be a lifelong, step-by-step building of a style of life and faith.

In the midst of a famous passage on love, the first theologian of the Christian Movement wrote: "When I grew up, I had finished with childish things." Writing of "the new relationship of grace" to the Christians in Rome, he invoked patience, "which

ON NURTURING CHRISTIANS

in turn develops a mature character, and a character of this sort produces a steady hope that will never disappoint us."

They also want other people to have it. They know from their own religious experience that they can't force other people to it and that they can't even give it to others. They can only offer it. But they know that their offer is made with help because God, at work in history and in human relationships, makes it too.

Paul put it to the Christians at Corinth who were arguing about the source of their religious experience. "I may have done the planting and Apollos the watering," he wrote, "but it was God who made the seed grow."

Christians are by definition a people who nurture. Their religious experience requires it and determines its nature.

My proposition is:

Nurturing is one of the things Christians can do best, and in doing it they have a gift to offer to the schools of the world.

It is a bold proposition, and the second part may seem even more presumptuous than the first.

PROLOGUE

Nurturing is defined by essential Christianity, of course, not by institutional Christianity. To make that distinction is not to say anything new, though making it seems to be resented more now than in any period since the late Middle Ages when Martin Luther made it and the world was changed. In the comfortably distant past, institutional Christianity has produced programs of forced mass baptism, martyrdom, and inquisition which were supposed to enhance the effectiveness of Christian education but which, with the supreme irony of historical justice, destroyed not only the programs but the kind of institution that produced them. In the last fifty years, not so comfortably far removed, institutional Christianity has grown more and more dependent upon public education for design and technique in Christian education. Now, hardly distinguishable from secular schooling, having committed the same grievous errors, it falls under the same judgments. Worse, Christian education has become a follower of alien principles, destroying itself by destroying its own special nature.

Christianity may claim to be the original situation in which the medium is the message. That is the impact of the incarnation: when, to put it simply, God most wanted to make himself known to his creatures, he sent a messenger to them who

9

ON NURTURING CHRISTIANS

was himself the message. It is the model for all education: let the content and the teaching and the method be congruent.

In Christian education it is blasphemy, therefore, for the medium to be a massage. It is possible for massaging to be an effective technique in the selling of cars, cigarettes, and cosmetics through mass media, though even there questions of taste and ethics are raised by the Christian model.

In essential Christianity, the message is love: sin-redeeming, man-reconciling, world-releasing Love. Not massaging love.

In essential Christianity, the medium is love: right-creating, humanity-completing, world-confronting Love. Not medial love.

In nurturing Christians, therefore, the project is initiating and maintaining a process of divine-human development in which the means and the ends are the same.

As to the second part of the proposition, that in nurturing Christians have a lesson to offer to the schools of the world, there is no claim that public school teachers and administrators should turn to the Average Sunday Morning Church School for

PROLOGUE

guidance. We have all seen what usually goes on there: harried untrained mothers and maiden aunts desperately attempting to control some small part of the reluctant child's wandering attention for nice stories about nice people who lived a nice long time ago. A claim may be made that there are some revolutionary things going on here and there in the name of Christian education. They tend to take place outside church buildings and Sundays in summer camps and experimental conferences. They also tend not to come to the attention of institutional executives, for nurturers have learned to be both quiet and modest about their best work in the interests of continuing it. It might even be said that the best Christian education today is "underground." But then, minority and sub rosa *status has frequently in history been the condition in which Christian nurturing has been most true to itself.*

What is claimed is that now may be a time for Christian educators to find their speciality again. And that secular education may be more ready to learn from it than religious education.

One place for Christian educators to begin their re-search for their speciality is in the secular schools, in imitation of which they lost it. In that case, it may be worth remembering that when modern secular education was born in the post-Reformation era in Europe, it was then a child of Christian education.

I. SCHOOLING ✤ ✤

Something significant is stirring in the schools. Not only those who are expected to think and talk about schools, the Educators, are telling us. The school people themselves, the classroom Teachers and the day-to-day Students, are telling us too.

Education is the thing we Americans do more than any other people. Today one out of every three of us is engaged, as administrators or teachers or learners, at one level or another, in formal schooling. Almost all of us go to school for twelve years of our lives, more than half of us for sixteen, many of us do special courses in skill and trade schools, and many more of us, off and on for the rest of our lives, go to

ON NURTURING CHRISTIANS

extension classes in everything from hobbies to foreign languages. All told, it is the largest single item in our private and public budgets, and there is no way to count the informal learning we do through television, magazines, newspapers, and daily living. It may even be that we do it better than anyone else in the world. Whatever their specialities, our overseas visitors almost always inquire about our schools, and professional school-watchers from abroad are almost invariably unprepared for the quantity, quality, freedom, experimentalism, and seriousness of our schools. When something is stirring in the schools, it is stirring close to where we live.

Stirring is the thing American schools do. Already in its relatively short history, American education has undergone redirection at least three times. The first revolution in public education was for *quantity*, and it began among the first generation of Americans to live under the Constitution. It was built on the several forms of colonial education specializing in preparing enough indigenous people to staff the essential professions to run a new country. It resulted from the acknowledgement that universal literacy and independent thought were the foundation of a functioning democracy. It was dedicated to the principle that education should begin as early as possible and be provided by the State to all citizens. The second revolution was for *equality*. Some say it began as late as the Supreme Court decisions of 1954 determining that separate educational

SCHOOLING

opportunity for different races was not equal. Others point back to the demand of the new mechanized industries of the 19th century and their demand for literate and imaginative workers who never came from and seldom achieved high social status. In any case, though this revolution is far from complete, the third has already begun. It is a drive for *quality*, and some say it began with the scare the Russians threw into Americans in 1957 with their successful launching of the first man-made earth satellite. Others remember New England educators like Horace Mann, who was impressed with the achievements of elitist education in Europe and determined to make education in the United States universal without losing quality, and John Dewey, who devoted himself to the production of a distinctively American educational quality characterized by imaginative problem-solving.

Something more is stirring now. Changes in the world outside the classroom are creating a new world in the classroom.

1. The Logic Breakthrough

The ways in which people think are being altered. Marshall McLuhan has been telling the egghead segments of our population for some time that logic is formed by the technology of preserving and communicating information, and whether or not he is right in all the permutations of his philosophy, Americans as a whole are becoming aware that something is indeed happening in their heads.

The oldest known method of recording information is the petrograph, a picture scratched on the rock wall of a protected cave. Some of these have survived an incredibly long time and are perhaps the surest evidence we have that human intelligence

SCHOOLING

existed in the skull fragments of manlike animals from that ancient period. Some of the pictures are also incredibly beautiful. A scant half-dozen lines identify without question a leaping, antler-bearing stag. A group of pictures tells where the quarry was found, how numerous it was and how the hunt was successfully consummated. Extensive tribal experiences of searching and tracking, locating and pursuing, cornering and killing, cooking and eating are condensed into pictures and the residue of knowledge preserved.

The pictograph is at the small end of a funnel which at its large end encompasses life, survival, and death. The pictorial symbol is the result of a logic characterized by gathering and focusing. It is an aesthetic way of thinking.

It may well have been that the first intention of the artist was only to preserve the memory of an event. Even so, the picture turned out to serve an even more significant purpose: on another day a band of hungry hunters found the cave and its pictures, read from them the possible location of the quarry, and successfully repeated the hunt. The symbol preserving knowledge had become a medium of communication. The second band of hunters placed the small end of their funnel of experience against the first band's condensation of experience and expanded from that focused picture to their own larger experience of forests and stags. It was not necessary that they meet the first band face to face. It was not even

ON NURTURING CHRISTIANS

necessary for them to know anything else of their existence but this picture. The symbol which was the result of gathering-and-focusing became a medium of communication by precipitating an application, though in reverse, of the original mode of thinking.

The invention of writing, millennia later, signified a change in all that. Writing is built on speech rather than on pictures. Though language at the beginning may well have been little more than audible pictures —isolated sounds representing running hooves or falling water—it eventually, through stages of development still untraceable, fell together in sequences of separable and identifiable words telling who was performing an action and the results.

The basic structure of language is linear, establishing a line of relationships between subject, action, and object. And when visual symbols for words were invented, through stages of development somewhat more traceable than the invention of speech, they tended to fall together in the same sort of linear sequences. That is, the writing was in continuous lines —up and down or horizontal—beginning at one point—top or bottom, right or left—and ending at another. The whole process is mental rather than aesthetic, and the logic of writing is also characterized by linear sequences. To write effectively, one must think linearly. Learning to read is not merely learning to recognize the symbols but also learning to think in lines. It is a difficult skill to acquire, even

SCHOOLING

after three millennia of practice requiring several years to teach.

For centuries, writing and reading were the medium of communication for only a small portion of the people, those who could afford the time to write material out by hand or those who could afford the money to own the result of the time-consuming work of others. They were the linear thinkers of Greece, Rome, and the Middle Ages, people who thought in major premise–minor premise–and conclusion, beginning-middle-and-end, cause-and-effect. But when the printing press and interchangeable type were invented in the 15th century of our era, reading became the medium of information and communication for everybody. Both religious reformation and scientific revolution rode on the printed page. Both were formed, propagated, and projected in linear modes of thinking. Since then the linearity of any assertion has been popularly—almost universally—accepted as the demonstration of its validity.

Many are now arguing that the most influential medium of communication in our world is no longer printing but television. McLuhan and others are arguing that a change in logic is occurring.

It is a truism, perhaps of Oriental origin, that a picture is worth many words, even in a book, because it activates a broader experience than words. Further, when the pictures can move in an approximation of actual events, a still more complex communication is possible. And when sound can be added

ON NURTURING CHRISTIANS

so that words are placed in their natural context rather than reduced to abstract symbols and fed through the eyes alone to the trained mind, the complexity and effectiveness increase immensely. The technology of television is often used as a symbol of the mode of thinking induced by it. In actual fact, the TV picture is a complex geometric mosaic of light and dark (or light and dark plus red, blue, and yellow) dots activated on the viewer's screen in response to a similar pattern of dots broadcast from the viewing camera in the television studio. But the viewer does not see dozens of discrete dots: he "sees" a picture, performing an instantaneous—and intuitive—integration of many separate stimuli into a single impression. A mind gathering information in this manner will think—will-he/nill-he—in a similar fashion, storing knowledge, relating data, and solving problems.

Now this is very unlike linear thinking. It is, indeed, called the multilinear mode of logic. Electronic circuitry is an example: a complex interweaving of wires (or more accurately, of routes) into a compound of simultaneous possible combinations which are put together instantly in response to key-stimulations producing a single result, and on another occasion, perhaps even with the same input, a different (though related) result.

The upshot of all this is the possibility—if not the actuality—that a generation which was formed in a world without television thinks—and perhaps even

SCHOOLING

feels—differently from a generation which was formed in a world with it. And if their logic is different, they will learn differently. They may find it much harder to learn to read. They may not see the point in learning to read. They may be frustrated by linear modes of logic. Using the same data as linear thinkers do, they may reach different conclusions with multilinear logic. They may even, given these technological circumstances, be right.

2. The Knowledge Explosion

The ways in which knowledge is treated are being altered. There was a time when it was possible for one person to know at least something about everything. As human history goes, that was not long ago. Aristotle may be cited among such geniuses. It remained possible through the medieval period, Thomas Aquinas seeming to be such a person. Michelangelo and Leonardo were types of "the Renaissance Mind." But after the Renaissance, the modern expansion of knowledge began. Experimentation, exploration, and communication added to the fund of human knowledge more rapidly than any single

SCHOOLING

mind could encompass. Books became storehouses, and for perhaps a century it was thought that a team of men could put everything into a series of books designed for that purpose. Encyclopedias and encyclopedists they were called. Then it became necessary to invent libraries in which to gather the multitude of books that no single person could acquire or keep. Then the libraries became so enormous that specialized collections were necessary. And now it is clear that information itself increases at a mind-boggling geometric rate (shall we say multilinear rather than linear?): every secret unlocked and each new datum uncovered releases a flood of new secrets and data, and each new element of the flood is interrelated with all the other elements both new and ancient as well as yet to come. And none of it is of any value unless it be available now and in relation to matters as yet unthought of. Memory and books have suddenly become archaic.

Electronic circuitry, that example of multilinear modes of logic, seems to provide the solution to the problem of knowledge storage. The first level of the solution comes through miniaturization: what the transistor is to radio and television, high reduction photography is to the printed page. It is now possible to print a half-dozen books—a thousand pages—on a single card three inches by five inches in size. It is called a supermicrofiche: the plain microfiche, now obsolete, would record only 60 to 100 pages on a 3x5 card. It is possible to fit 250 of these cards into the space occupied by an ordinary book. One project, called *The Library of American Civilization*, will contain 20,000 volumes numbering about six million pages—ordinarily requiring 2,000 feet of library shelf space—in 32 trays 16 inches long. The cost is about $21,000 compared to the $450,000 required to buy it in book form. A viewer will cost about $150, and "hard-copy printouts" of any page may be made almost instantly. Plans are already under way for more materials and installations in an interlocked system of strategically located libraries.

Electronic circuitry is also solving the problem of information retrieval. "Data Banks," based on computer cards, have been in operation for some time at several of our more advanced technological institutes. A student may avail himself of computer service for course-related data at any time of the day or night, sometimes no more distant than the end of his dormitory hallway. The *New York Times*' Information Bank is using miniaturized photography of its files. Involved in the system is a complex of IBM computers, a high-speed printer, a microfiche storage and retrieval device controlled by another computer, and both video screen and hard-copy printer terminals. The *Times* calls it "the first fully automated system for the retrieval of general information." University Microfilms is now engaged in a pilot project designed to index about 35 periodicals and to feed its information into a data bank: included will be title, author, and several subject headings cross-referenced,

SCHOOLING

with separate listings for poems, films, and books. The extension to films and recordings through cassette packaging is only a step away. The time is not far off, a telephone company advertisement indicates, when children in local schools and their homes can secure information, visit with Leonard Bernstein, hear Robert Frost read poetry, and be guided to the solution of mathematical problems by using a Touch-Tone* phone.

The upshot of the geometric expansion and immediate availability of knowledge is the possibility that education may soon be able to concentrate on the tools for evaluating and applying knowledge rather than on the methods of acquiring it. That is a task it has not been able to undertake for at least a couple of centuries. Memorizing need no longer be at the center of learning because it has become futile. We may have reason to worry that memory may become a lost art and that children may become more expert at key-punching than at problem-solving, but whether or not schools and teachers re-evaluate their aims and standards. it is clear that technology is catching up so rapidly that the classroom may soon be a very different place from the one we once knew and loved or endured.

3. The Communication Marvel

The ways in which people relate are being altered. The present adult generation is the first in history to have lived its entire life in a world where it was possible to communicate instantly everywhere in the world. The radios of their childhood were primitive affairs. But in spite of fading and static, they were there when Tunney knocked out Dempsey and Calvin Coolidge assumed the presidency. The news security systems of World War II provided an important section of the world's population for the first time with the consciousness of what it is not to know what is going on at that moment in faraway

SCHOOLING

places. Since then, a generation has been nurtured into young adulthood with pictures in the living room at dinner time of the earth quaking in the Middle East, their brothers fighting in Southeast Asia, and explorers walking on the moon.

The result is that nowhere are people necessarily strangers to people anywhere. Instant mass communication has done more to inform people everywhere about one another than several centuries of exploration, travel, and diplomacy. Illiterate and almost culture-less Africans on the floating reed islands of mysterious Lake Chad know a great deal about Europe and America.

The relation also seems to be direct. Significance does not depend upon history—the accounts of how one got to where he is, speaks as he does, and acts in certain ways—so much as upon the simultaneity itself, wherein both share what they are now saying and doing. Relation does not depend upon added information or a third person's interpretation or mediation. The simultaneous appeal to sight and sound creates the sense of actual presence. It is much more like the relationship of the primitive tribal village of the rain forest than that of the sophisticated modern city in which next-door neighbors are strangers and self-chosen walls of anonymity keep people moving past each other in well lubricated channels without ever really seeing or contacting one another. Contrasted to the result of reading paragraphs of description in a book, this relationship is a living one.

ON NURTURING CHRISTIANS

One can experience how it would feel to be there, acting and speaking with these people who can no longer therefore be described as strangers.

This is clearly a different kind of relationship between persons than those relations which are produced by living together over an extended period of time. This new relation may be two-way, but it is not mutual; that is to say, each person may extend himself to the other and come across to the other, but there is no possibility that the persons will meet each other and modify their extensions in terms of each other. It may be significant that the denizens of Lake Chad who know a great deal about Europe and America have no desire to go there.

This new relation is always also limited, if not by the operator behind the camera lens at least by the nature of the lens itself: for example, a lens does not have the wide angle of vision that the human eye does and cannot "see around" a subject or situation; for another example, the lens can focus attention on a subject with far more concentration than can the human eye. The point is not whether the lens sees more or less effectively than the eye so much as that it sees differently. The senses omitted from this new relation are the more intimate ones: sight and hearing are brought into play, but smell and touch are not. The new relation between persons is therefore built on the more abstract senses: the issue is not whether it is more complete than knowledge gained by reading or less complete than relation built

SCHOOLING

on mutual presence, but the kind of relation that results when it is sustained by the senses of seeing and hearing. It may be significant that young people nurtured on television violence do not seem to know that knifing and shooting hurt.

The upshot of the establishment of instantaneous mass communication throughout much of the world may well change the classroom from a smallish rectangular cubicle on Elm Street to the world itself. With equipment for tapping mass media in the classroom, distance may no longer be a negative dimension in learning. The familiar study of Current Events may become a class in Immediate Events. The instruction of the most informed and interesting specialists on a host of subjects may be available to any class anywhere. Mass media techniques for achieving geographical nearness are already being applied to time: not only the artifacts but the life of ancient periods may come alive in the classroom. As a result, the relation between teacher and learner may be modified because the teacher is no longer required to be the personal source of knowledge and expertise for the class. And, perhaps, in a new generation which has spent its conscious life in the world of mass media, the relation among students may become tribal, direct, and two-dimensional.

4. The School Revolt

The attitudes of classroom people are being altered. The historic revolutions in American education seem to have been conceived and led by the Educators. What is stirring in education now appears to have its center in teaching-and-learning itself. Things, some as yet unguessed, are happening to persons as a result of the Logic Breakthrough, The Knowledge Explosion, and The Communication Marvel. It would appear that teachers and learners are beginning to exercise their own influence on an enterprise preparing learners for a future they sense adults cannot even imagine.

There are many, though yet uncoordinated, stirrings.

SCHOOLING

A process sometimes called "escalation downward" is stirring. The term seems to have been invented by young adults working with teen-agers in runaway centers and the like. Working at helping alienated parents and children to understand each other, they observed that values are in the process of moving into lower age groups. The values of last decade's college student are the values of today's high schooler; the values of today's high schooler are in the process of becoming the values of tomorrow's children. Language is one example: the four-letter vocabulary of World War II infantrymen was adopted by the college student of the 50s, the high schooler of the 60s, and is now being heard among elementary school students. The drug scene is another example. One may also cite physiological facts: GIs of WWII were larger and more mature physically than the doughboys of WWI; puberty is arriving earlier than ever before, now at 10 and 11 years of age rather than at 13 and 14; boy's voices change three years earlier than they did 20 years ago; in 1970 the fin whale began to mate at six years of age, whereas in 1948 he began at ten years of age. And further, in the process of moving downward in age, the intensity with which the values are held is escalated. The clue was that children were coming to the runaway centers earlier and the average age of "street people" was lowering.

A rebellion against authority in education is stirring. Revolt against implacable authority is nothing new, but it has a new flavor in American education.

ON NURTURING CHRISTIANS

Revolt by students in schools is especially difficult to muster. Student rebels are heavily outnumbered by school supporters, that is, the phalanxes of teachers and administrators in the public schools and their own parents at home. Further, a student's entire and mysterious future was made to appear to depend upon successful adjustment now to the school and its present demands. And, finally, in American public schools the philosophy expertly repeated by teachers everywhere was that education is democracy and democracy is progressive.

As a result, it was in higher education, where students are most independent, closest to their own futures, and have the longest perspective on the rate of democratic change, that rebellion first flared. Campus uprisings—for example, the Free Speech Movement at the University of California in Berkeley in 1964—can no longer be dismissed as a modern version of adolescent high jinks. The escalation is downward: in the 30s the campus radical was a full professor, in the 50s the campus radical was an associate professor, in the 60s he was a graduate student or TA, recently he is among the freshmen and sophomores.

In any case, it was on the university campuses that the educational revolt surfaced, and it came from a coagulation of values held by teachers and students rather than by administrators, trustees, and parents. The catalyst was too many endless registration lines and IBM cards, enormous classes and overflow rooms

SCHOOLING

with remote-TV lectures, Tuesday Deans, absentee department chairmen, and closed office doors.

The new set of values did not run along traditional lines, distinguishing between scientists and humanists, rich and poor, old and young, black and white. The new set of values tended to give preference to personal rights over property rights, to human needs over technological requirements, to cooperation over competition, to distribution over concentration, to consumer over producer, to ends over means, to openness over secrecy, to personal expression over social forms, to gratification over striving. It was, in short, an often amorphous though clear-cut challenge to a scarcity-oriented, technology-controlled, authority-dominated, de-personalized preparation for a long-postponed adult life. By the time it came, it seemed to 20- and 30-year-old students, there would be nothing left to live for. Individuals dropped out, into drugs and occultism: their choice of alternatives was an evidence in itself. Others stayed, letting their hair grow on their heads, faces, and armpits as a visible sign of a shaky declaration of independence. But gradually it appeared that something identifiable as a counter-culture was forming and that it might well contain the forms of the future.

The universities, having bred the protean counter-culture, became the first scene of its clash with the prior operative-culture. Both old and new are present on campus. It is the one place in society where older men and women expose themselves systematically and professionally to the young. It is the one place in society where the young go to listen regularly and sometimes respectfully to the older. On every campus one of the major buildings is the library, in which are stored the wisdom and problem-solutions of the past. On every campus there is another building which houses the laboratories in which the problems of the future are being solved. It is supported by the institutions of the past, it is inhabited by the citizens of the future. It cannot ignore the new culture as the rest of society can do if it wishes. It cannot simply accommodate to the new without losing the support of the old and going bankrupt.

It may be important to note that while the clash has often been destructive, the outcome promises to be constructive. Because the old and new are so explosively present to each other in the university, the only way for life to continue is for a *new* new to be made possible through interaction with and transformation of the old. It is no accident that Charles Reich, in *The Greening of America*, sees Consciousness III as simultaneously made possible by Consciousness II and I and replacing Consciousness II and I. The thesis developed, as he says, in five years of conversation with students and colleagues at Yale. It is the way schoolroom people tend to think.

It may be equally important to notice that the crisis in the universities is moving downward into the public secondary and elementary schools. Many

SCHOOLING

of the identified rock-throwers on college campuses in recent springs have been high school students. However, the institutional agony of the public schools is perhaps more indicative: to meet the demands of rising enrollments school districts have been pouring huge sums into building programs at the same time that social demographers were telling us that the number of students will decline sharply in the 70s; the tax burdens on the public are becoming so heavy that voters are refusing to make new money available, not discriminating between building programs and educational programs; fewer and fewer new teachers are being recruited into the public school systems at precisely the time when it appears that many of the older teachers are unable to keep pace with the technological revolutions in thinking, knowing, and communicating; more and more gifted teachers are being moved into administrative posts which require a different set of skills entirely from those of the classroom in which they have demonstrated superiority. Simultaneously, the prestigious Conant Reports were telling us that what we needed was more buildings of the same sort and higher salaries for the same teachers. While university students were rebelling against the depersonalization of higher education, the manufacturers of electronic hardware began buying textbook publishing houses and mounting advertising campaigns in the expectation of selling the public schools huge quantities of computers, TV sets, and machines for programmed learning.

With the downward movement has come an escalation of the educational critique. In the late 50s and early 60s, the confusion in the schools bred a revolt against racial segregation, or outdated curricula, or ineffective teaching methods, or halfhearted teachers, or high competition spurred by grades. For the past five years a different sort of analysis has been taking shape. It has been vocalized by John Holt, Herbert Kohl, Jonathan Kozol, George Dennison. What the schools teach most of all, they say, is the importance of schooling. The school sets out to equip the child with a ready-made psyche for use in a ready-made world. The children's resistance has given rise to the educational assumption that children are improperly cared for at home, lazy by nature, and must be continually prodded by the public school, threatened if necessary, to learn anything. The schools have thus robed themselves in a sort of unchallengeable priesthood, protecting the national destiny against subtle but preventable self-destruction. Paul Goodman has called for a radicalization of the schools. Ivan Illich has appealed for the de-schooling of society and the dis-establishment of the schools. The revolt has turned against the institution itself.

At issue is the American assumption that progress toward a better world is guaranteed by the schools. Near the beginning of the 20th century, John Dewey reformed the classical schools of America by popu-

SCHOOLING

larizing the theory that the school was democracy in miniature and that the secret of democracy was constant change. By the beginning of the last third of the century, however, the second proposition had been lost entirely, and what remained was a hidden though official assumption that the school provided the only route of initiation into established society. Public schools held an absolute monopoly on this function: children were regarded as newcomers who must go through a naturalization process in order to belong. The process consumed about 15,000 hours of the candidate's time, preempting most of his childhood and adolescent years, assembled in groups of about thirty, under the authority of teachers trained in and certified by the same system, who by their behavior exuded convictions that education is valuable only when it is achieved in required schools, that success depends on the amount of learning consumed, and that learning about the world is better than learning from it, though frequently they said different things about the meaning of education. Only diplomaed products of the system may be admitted to full citizenship, and then only after about three years of further schooling in the same sort of system, or an internship in full-time employment, or war experience.

This sort of schooling appears to work quite well for two kinds of students. One is the youngster of a single outstanding gift: he knows what he wants in education for there are no competitors within himself for his loyalty; he is a self-motivated learner because he can be counted on to teach himself what he needs to learn to satisfy his single capacity, whatever the size of the class or the efficiency of the teacher or the subject of the course. The other for whom the system works is the child of modest all-round gifts: he fits well because he does not have the intellect to be overly critical; he is not outstanding in any subject so he learns early to please the teacher in lieu of mastering the subject, cooperating with her wishes and later manipulating the high school system so as to get the most out of it. Both kinds are excellent candidates for machine teaching and programmed learning, the one because they are so bright that they do not need to accept packaged learning as their only route to knowledge and the other because their modest capacities are so preoccupied by keeping up that they have neither the energy nor insight to evaluate what is happening to them. Both are deep into system-pleasing extracurricular activities, the one because, not being overly challenged by the required work, they have interest and energy to spare, and the other because, not having the motivation to challenge the go-go of school spirit and the like, they invest themselves deeply. Both will make the records to get into college, and when they graduate they will go on to become the thinkers and managers of the businesses and governments of the United States, both of which are highly canalized systems as well.

This sort of schooling does not appear to work well

SCHOOLING

for two other kinds of students. One is the youngster with high all-round capacity and therefore none outstanding. He places in the 95th percentile or better in the aptitude tests. But since he does not possess one isolated capacity in the high range, he tends not to be self-motivated about any of his high range capacities, and because he is intellectually acute he tends to be critical of those who do channel well and of the system itself. He clearly has the capacity for higher education, but he may never be challenged by unimaginative teachers or turned on by the subjects they delumine, and he may never get himself sufficiently organized to get to college. The other is the child of minimal gifts, say below the 75th percentile in the aptitude tests, and he is early designated by his school guidance counselors as "not college material." Now, both of these types are the freer spirits of the younger generation: they do not fit the style of the schools. But they outnumber the channeled students, and on them the future depends: on the relatively few students of high all-round capacity because they are precisely the sort who have the capacity for the interdisciplinary and imaginative thinking that will characterize post-technological society; and on the less-than-gifted because they are "the masses" of tomorrow on whose capacity to exist in the global village its very possibility depends.

5. Alternative Schooling

The alarm comes from inside the schools and has been growing rapidly. Parents who have listened day by day to their own children's reports of school classroom experiences have turned up, not at PTA meetings and Back-to-School demonstrations to hear the party line, but in the classrooms during regular school hours. They were surprised to find that classrooms looked like the place they had gone to school but felt very different. They saw for themselves the boredom, fear, and lack of learning that too often accompany schooling, not only for the poor and the black but for suburban white youngsters as well. Educators who have listened semester after semester

SCHOOLING

to their students' reports of practice-teaching experiences have described the authoritarianism and joylessness of many classrooms under established teachers, the stress on achievement and discipline at the expense of learning, the suppression of the natural curiosity and instincts of the young.

The search for another educational system is on.

Some parents and educators have experimented with variations of the present school system. One revolves about some sort of *voucher plan,* which would ideally enable every child to attend whatever school his parents chose for him. English schools provide a working model. In the United States it would be necessary to send with the pupil a voucher entitling his school to the amount of money appropriated per pupil in the local school budget. This could, of course, work to the advantage of schools outside the public school system, but the hope of most educators is that the plan would stimulate the public school bureaucracies by ending their local monopolies and exposing them to competition. Another variation proposes a system of *child-care centers* extending from age two or even younger to the upper primary level and providing every child with a combination of services to assure optimum physical, mental, emotional, and social development. Head-Start and Follow-Through programs are cited as pilots of such a program. Intellectual development and self-motivation are believed to follow as a consequence of a suitably nurturing environment in which the child finds opportunity, stimulation, and reward. A third variation advocates *schools without walls*. Proponents regard "the process of schooling" as more important than the place and hold that learning comes most profitably from experience in a variety of circumstances, exposures, and involvements. Programs in some Eastern city centers, notably Philadelphia, are cited as examples. The community becomes the school, and whoever knows what the pupil wants to learn becomes his teacher. This is, of course, precisely the way most of us have learned the greater part of what we know.

All three variations of the present educational system have, however, run into significant difficulties. The voucher plan has become a partisan political issue, for one thing, and for another has been backed by people who sound more like lobbyists with vested interests than like educational reformers. The child-care plan has apparently sounded to some like a communist plot and has unfortunately appealed to some school administrators who endorse the contention that all children don't need schools and that exceptional behavior on the part of a child is clear evidence that the public interest is best served by excluding him from normal public schools. And the school-without-walls proposal has divided the theorists into arguing about whether the community actually does possess the power to teach, and some parents are agitated about why Johnny isn't doing the college prep course.

SCHOOLING

Other parents and educators have struck out on their own to develop an actual alternative, another or new kind of school that will allow new forms of education. The New Schools, or Free Schools, or Community Schools—they go by all these names—have sprung up by the hundreds across the country in the last five years. They charge little or no tuition, are frequently held together by spit and string, and run mainly on the energy and excitement of people who have set out to do their own thing. The variety seems limitless. They range from inner-city to suburban and rural white. Some seem to be pastoral escapes from the grit of modern conflict, and are pretty grubby by any 20th-century American standard of convenience and cleanliness. Others are deliberate experiments in urban plunging: multi-cultural, multi-racial, multi-lingual. And some of them look pretty grubby, too. They turn up anywhere: in city storefronts, Co-op garages, old barns, abandoned barracks, church buildings, parents' homes. They have wildly irresponsible but ingenuously transparent names: Someday School, Viewpoint Non-School, A Peck of Gold, The New Community, New Directions, or simply, "The School." The names reflect the two things they most often have in common: the idea of freedom for youngsters and a humane education.

The Community School of Santa Barbara states in its brochure: "The idea is that freedom is a supreme good; that people, including young people,

ON NURTURING CHRISTIANS

have a right to freedom, and that people who are free will in general be more open, more humane, more intelligent than people who are directed, manipulated, ordered about." Dedicated to children, they take seriously Jean Piaget's dictum that "play is the serious business of childhood." And at times the visitor finds the school to be a veritable Garden of Eden or Second Coming, depending on whether he happens to be a disciple of Jean Rousseau or John the Revelator. English experiments in Leicestershire and at Summerhill have exercised tremendous influence. At a table is a group of children struggling to build arches out of sugar cubes; another two or three children are working with an Erector set, others with tape recorders and a typewriter. In the midst of all this independent activity is one teacher helping one child learn to write his name. The picture is reminiscent of the classrooms in John Dewey's University of Chicago Experimental School in 1896.

It is significant, however, that the mortality rate is high among these alternative schools. The average life-span is estimated to be about eighteen months, and the route to that rather quick death seems to be fairly typical.

The first crisis is financial. Most schools are started by people who are not rich and charge little or no tuition. After all, the rich have always had alternatives. Teachers work for little more than pennies, and sometimes they are not paid at all. "I found a nice landlord who doesn't bug me about the rent," said

SCHOOLING

one teacher. "I dip into my savings, and get my parents and my friends to invite me to dinner. Then there are food stamps." Even teachers cannot live on $200 a month. And the constant struggle for fiscal survival too often takes precedence over education.

The second crisis is emotional. There is almost always a certain amount of red tape, harassment by various bureaucracies, and even public hostility. In Salt Lake City, for example, a citizens' committee tried to close a new Summerhill School on the grounds that the school was immoral and the teachers were Communists. Working with children in an open classroom with few guidelines makes tremendous and often unexpected demands on the teachers. The concept of free, ecstatic education can be forcefully and imaginatively verbalized, but actualizing it day after day requires enormous reserves of joy, love, and mutual trust. "If you stop putting the pressure on the kids, the tendency is to stop putting pressure on the staff, too," one teacher observed. Schools that fail within a few months of opening tend to be those begun by people merely interested in trying out something new. When the idea turns out to be more complex and its implementation more difficult than expected, the original good feeling evaporates and a deeper determination is demanded.

The third crisis is spiritual. If the school makes it over the financial hurdles and survives the emotional struggle, it soon encounters the deeper problems.

ON NURTURING CHRISTIANS

This often takes the form of "structure" *versus* "nonstructure." Having experimented with the idea of freedom, and having discovered its inherent difficulties, many parents become impatient and anxious. Are the children learning anything, they wonder, and does it matter? Frequently there is a slowdown in the acquisition of traditional academic skills. Children, it turns out, *had* rather play than learn to spell, and the blossoming forth of innate genius in a warm, benevolent atmosphere fails to occur. Anxious adults begin to argue for more structure to the school day, more direction for the kids, more emphasis on the familiar Three Rs. Others insist on maintaining the freedom, and upon "learning to work with children on a new freer basis that really tests its limitations and possibilities." If a school survives the argument of principles, it is often reorganized and emerges from the fires of crisis a strong and self-directed educational process. But, more often than not, the school does not survive and the parents shamefacedly trail their youngsters back to the public school they had left hopefully last fall.

6. A Stirring of Spirit

The upshot of all the revolt in the schools is the possibility that what is stirring there is not moving deeply enough. Critiques by school people seem to be limited by the perspectives and principles of the schools themselves. The philosophical understanding of what is needed to become human is often too cautious, like the proposed variations of the present school system; the reforms of education are too often insufficiently grounded in reality, like the alternative schools; when bold understanding and realistic reforms do exist, they have not yet been related to each other.

Some classroom people grasp the need for a

changed environment for learning. They call in the subcontractors and spend all summer renovating and innovating. In the fall the place smells of new paint, and doors are in new places. When a new building is needed, different architects are summoned and a building with circular walls and resource centers and programmed audio-visuals is constructed. But during the heavy winter days the restlessness continues.

Some educational planners dream of schedules and modules and curricular innovations. But their talk is of "materials" and "techniques." "What do you want most from students?" a planner was asked. "Respect," he said, "and their utmost effort." "But all they seem to want is love and a sense of humor." The planner's eyes lit up. "I see," he said, "you mean positive feedback." Having glimpsed, perhaps, what the young want for life, educators turn it into academic jargon and the students sink back into their accustomed midafternoon boredom.

Some alternative school people have been incisive in pointing out that public school people are too busy with institutional matters and preoccupied with professional interests to think about the experience of being educated. But when they have withdrawn from the public schools to invent schools of their own, they, too, have focused on what they think the children want or ought to have. And so they design schools characterized by freedom, never asking the kids themselves whether they want freedom, or,

SCHOOLING

more difficult, what sort of freedom it is that they want and what sort of discipline. By Christmas the place is falling apart.

There are ways of trying to find out what the learners themselves really want and need. The scientists of education work very hard at it with their sociological and psychological instruments. They tell us that the young of today want to be freed from the tyranny of roles. They are probably right. So the adults open up the classroom a bit. Students use the teacher's first name. They roam the room, go ungraded, choose their own texts. It's better than before, but in the spring the rocks are flying again.

When we listen, the young seem to be saying that what they want is much more profound than redecoration or feedback: not techniques but qualities of the soul; not freedom so much as daring, warmth, wit, imagination, honesty, loyalty, grace, resilience. Can these things be taught? They cannot be programmed, that's for sure. They seem to be learned, when they are, in activity and communion—in the sharing of personhood.

A student was arguing the need for burning things down and trashing windows. "What else," she said, "can I do?" Who really knows? Perhaps try to get to the bottom of things, try to see clearly what we all need. "But when I see clearly," she said, "I freak out." That's why we need friends. "But," she said, beginning to cry, "I have no friends."

It would appear that what the young want—and

ON NURTURING CHRISTIANS

at the same time, perhaps, are awed by—is a kind of spiritual renaissance: the ability to live decently and responsibly beyond the minimal limits of current definitions of survival, and the ability to provide for one's fellows enough help to sustain them. What saves us as human beings is a kind of mutual gift: the transforming quality of acts and lives. This is the kind of knowledge that is difficult to come by formally because it almost always comes spontaneously. It is therefore always threatening to break in and disrupt everything that *is* being taught.

At this level, at least, the situation is no different than it was—and is?—for today's adults. And it is no different from the situation explored so sensitively by the ancient Hebrews and called revelation, experienced by the early Christians and called redemption. Paul Goodman says that it is very much like 1510 when Luther went to Rome. It is perhaps even more like 1212 when the children of central Europe trooped off on their own Crusade to the Holy Land.

But the kids think that we don't know. They are battered by the world they think their parents chose and their teachers are dedicated to preserving, and they see it as a mixture of yearning and savagery, despair and exhilaration, gentleness and violence, grasping for paradise lost and demand for paradise now, a reaching that in its desperate grabbiness precludes the possibility of ever possessing.

Apocalyptic language ought, probably, to be avoided as much as possible. One should be very

SCHOOLING

careful before he proclaims that the present crisis has no genuine predecessors. But if this is not the kingdom of the apocalypse, it is at least an apocalyptic condition of the soul. Our present generation of learners is the child of that condition. They seem to know that something is stirring really deep down. There is every evidence that they feel desperate about it, and are trying to do for themselves what they think in their innocence their elders have never tried very hard to do.

INTERLOGUE ✦ ✦

1. Christian Education

If Christian educators were to do what their subject matter seems to imply, they would be doing some stirring of their own.

There are ways in which the churches can help the schools. Importantly, perhaps.

The churches have many educational buildings constructed during the "return to religion" of the 50s which are now too large for the Sunday school and stand unused *during most of the rest of the week. Many of them are well designed, often on public school specifications, for churches let public school architects as well as public school philosophers do much of their work for them during that halcyon period. In some churches which, often for financial rather than philosophical reasons, did not follow public school thinking, the demand for multiple use in church facilities produced educational spaces more attractive and flexible for a variety of learning activities than many public school classrooms. They are often located in areas that have changed economically and sociologically since they were built, areas which now never have enough facilities or finances for public schools. There are inner city areas where the church's buildings would be a tremendous assistance to the community's schools.*

There are ways in which the churches could supplement the public school revolution. Churches could supply all the advantages of an alternative school experience for children educated principally in less flexible public school programs—after school hours in the afternoon or evening or on Saturdays. Personal tutoring could be put into practice almost immediately. Most churches have the facilities and many have the expertise to offer special learning experiences in the arts, especially Protestantism's own art form,

INTERLOGUE

music: lessons on the largely unused pianos scattered through the building, and on the organ; singing lessons by the church musicians, singly and in groups by the choir people. Many churches could offer instruction in the other arts: dance, painting, theater. They could provide supplemental work in the humanities: history and philosophy for high schoolers, adding the religious dimension to the public school's necessarily secularized curriculum.

More importantly, Christian educators have a chance to make their own educational revolution. Any day of the week. Even on Sunday.

Christian educators should be an independent breed of thinkers. They have an independent stance. The apocalyptic condition of the soul is their natural ground. Personhood is their special business. They therefore might find themselves cutting right across the ways in which general education seems to be responding to the stirrings going on in the world and in the schools.

♣

They could well be with *The Logic Breakthrough. Public school people tend to go with the linear logic in which they were trained to think as educators: their modes of thinking about solutions to educational problems tend to be linear if for no other reason than that the problems are almost always defined in linear terms. They are, after all, the products of four hundred years or so of linear educational thinking. And, further, their entire professional life is lived in a linear, hierarchical system. But multilinear thinking is the natural ground of religion: only post-Reformation religion rode on the printed book; public medieval flowering of religion was nurtured in a less modern and linear culture; and both Christianity and Judaism sprang out of pre-linear experience.*

⚜

They could well be ambivalent *about The Knowledge Explosion. Religion is not interested in knowledge packages so much as in wisdom. Religious scholarship cares as passionately as any other sort about data and accuracy, but the purpose of scholarship is not so much merely more information as more insight. This is closely related, of course, to problem-solving, but it is not the same. Religious educators are more interested in the release of creativity than in the application of information to predefined puzzles. "In the beginning God created the heavens and the earth," and then, as another creative act, he turned the process*

INTERLOGUE

over to his creatures to continue. Christian educators are dedicated to deepening mystery and increasing human capacity to stand at its edge unafraid. In their classrooms they do not care to teach about life so much as to join their students in its spiritual issues.

♣

They could well stand aside from The Communication Marvel. Christian educators tend to have their own understanding of communication. It is not technological. They know that it is impossible to communicate without technology. Each teacher ordinarily wants to be as effective as possible and to find his own best techniques. But technological overload on communication destroys the personal qualities of its content. The nature of the religious subject matter suggests that this is disaster. Religious communication is not unilateral. It cannot only be watched or received. It is a two-way process, at minimum. Revelation is always a meeting, never merely a message. It is a contagion of the heart.

♣

They could well move beyond The School Revolt. Christian educators should be an independent breed of school people. They have never really been submerged in the institutionalism and jargon of the profes-

ON NURTURING CHRISTIANS

sional secular educators. (Their own leaders have tried often enough to sound like the education professionals, but it has never quite come off in the first-Monday-night teachers' meetings at the corner of Main and Maple.) Though there is institutionalized bureaucracy aplenty in church organizations, it has never really been effective in the church school classroom. (This is a fact sometimes mourned in Boston, Philadelphia, and Nashville, but almost always enjoyed in Paducah and Mason City.) They can never be very convincing as authority figures. (The Spirit of God "listeth where it wills" like the wind, with which it was synonymous in the Old Testament.) They have seldom if ever given grades. (How, after all, does one evaluate religious experience competitively?) Their classes have always been small. (It has been a blessing sometimes reluctantly accepted but effectively preventing the relationships in the church school classroom from becoming like those of mass education.) They have always been amateurs. (That is, they are amo-amas-amat people, who teach for the love of it, since there is never any pay and seldom much prestige.)

⚜

Whether or not today's Christian educators know it, they have been preparing for

INTERLOGUE

today's opportunity for a long time. The religious quest is as old as the human spirit. Two millennia of Western scholarship have provided the syllabus. Over three centuries of experiment in the New World with the relation of religious and general learning have supplied techniques. A century of the Christian Education Movement has developed a spiritualized philosophy of education. It may be ironic that Christian education has begun to get it all together just at the time when the churches appear to be retrenching; it may be important that Christian education is getting ready to move at a time when the schools are in crisis and the people in a state of metaphysical hunger.

In any case, Christian education has its own thing to do. It is, now as always, nurturing Christians.

2. Christian Teaching

In nurturing Christians, teaching is a soul-making thing to do.

It shakes one up. It takes one's breath away and gives it back clean and fresh. It demands never-ending makeup work. It is the beginning of the world.

⚜

It begins in the most common human activity. Whether it is more original than the solitary struggle for survival is a matter for debate, but it probably is. At any rate, it is universal: giving-and-receiving.

INTERLOGUE

Dynamically, it is not unlike giving and receiving a cold ripe watermelon. A dozen eggs. 83¢. A perfumed letter. A mirror. A handtissue. A drink of water. A meal. A handshake. An embrace. A carved wooden box.

Dear Pat,

> You came upon me carving some kind of little figure out of wood, and you said:
> "Why don't you make something for me?"
> I asked what you wanted, and you said, "A box."
> "What for?"
> "To put things in."
> "What things?"
> "Whatever you have," you said.
> Well, here's your box. Nearly everything I have is in it, and it's not full. Pain and excitement are in it, and feeling good or bad, and evil thoughts and good thoughts— the pleasure of design and some despair and the indescribable joy of creation. And on top of all these are the gratitude and love I have for you.
> And still the box is not full . . .
>
> John

The letter is addressed to Paschal Covici. It is signed "John." The last name is Steinbeck. The box he made for Pat: East of Eden.

ON NURTURING CHRISTIANS

It takes two to give and receive. No one ever gives anything away without a receiver. No one ever received anything without a giver.

It takes skill to give. Nothing was ever received unless it was given in such a way that it could be accepted.

It takes skill to receive. Nothing was ever given unless it was received in such a way that it could be given away.

The significance of the gift lies as much in the giving-and-receiving as in the object itself. Yet, there could never be giving-and-receiving without a gift.

One cannot speak of teaching Christianity without speaking of learning.

⚜

Teaching and learning Christianity is a special kind of giving-and-receiving. It is not an accident. It is an event, not merely a happening. It is giving-and-receiving raised to the level of intentionality.

It rests on the differences between people. One is older than the other. One has experienced something different from what the other has. One knows more than the

INTERLOGUE

other. One has seen more than the other. One is aware, and the other is not. Without differences it would not occur. Teaching and learning do not happen between people who are exactly alike. But then, no two people are exactly alike.

It begins with an offer. The offer may be either to give or to receive. Either the student or the teacher may initiate teaching, and it may arise almost imperceptibly from the stream of life, but it does not begin without a gesture, an act.

It has to do with a special kind of gift. The gift is chosen. At the beginning it is seldom something new, but it is always something more. To those who have common sense it is wisdom. To those who have wisdom it is love. To those who have love it is the incarnation. To those who have the incarnation it is common sense. When it is something more to both, it is indeed something new. It is both inside and outside to them both. It is both subjective and objective to them both.

Because teaching is intentional, teaching and learning often have something to do with set times and places, but not necessarily. It is often planned and prepared, but not always. It often has a goal in view, but it may not be reached; it may be redirected, and when the end does come the goal may be unexpected.

There is something personally creative about raising a common human activity from the running deeps of the soul to the level of intentionality.

⚜

Teaching and learning Christianity is intentional giving-and-receiving conducted at an intuitional level.

It is a fragile thing. Without sensitivity it cannot exist.

The differences between people cannot be closed. They must not be obscured. In both cases personhood is destroyed. The differences, however, may be crossed. In that case personhood is enhanced.

Crossing the chasm between one's own ground of experience and another's is a risky adventure.

Sometimes it is best begun in a formal relationship. The teacher knows who he is and what he is expected to do. The learner knows who he is and what he is expected

INTERLOGUE

to do. There is no threat to either. But teaching will not occur unless formality is transcended and the risks accepted.

Standing on another's ground of experience requires his permission. He has the right to refuse. He often does. He often withdraws it even after it has been given. Learning works best, therefore, in response to an invitation. The basic technique in teaching is inducing an invitation. And in keeping it alive.

Standing across the chasm is an act full of grace. It means standing on another's side of experience without leaving one's own and without displacing the other. To stand all on one side would be either to lose one's identity or to swallow up the other's. These are occupational hazards for both teachers and learners.

It is a grace-full act because it means experiencing the experience of receiving by the other. A teacher is one who always knows, even when he is teaching, what it is to be a learner. In teaching this is a primary law, elsewhere it is an exception.

It is a grace-full act because it means bearing the gift in one's own person. A teacher is one on whose face are written the sorrows and joys of one who has seen more than his pupils. In religion this is a fundamental function, elsewhere it is a rarity.

⚜

Teaching and learning Christianity is an action completed by an act in kind.

Mutuality is the essence. It is also the result.

Teaching and learning Christianity form a special relationship. It is dynamic: two living beings meet across their differences. It is complex: each is in relation to one who is not himself. It is delicate: each finds himself limited by the other but not bound by the other.

It is complete only when the action of giving-and-receiving is conducted by both the giver and the receiver at the same time, the giver being simultaneously a receiver and the receiver simultaneously a giver.

Then it is complete because both are exposed to another giving-and-receiving beyond them both. Christians call it God. They see in Jesus Christ God's own supremely risky and graceful act of giving-and-

INTERLOGUE

receiving. They understand the whole dynamic, complex, and delicate relationship to be love. They know from having experienced it that participating in it is creative of a more abundant personhood.

The learner is induced by the act of giving and receiving to risk the acceptance of divine love, an act which induced the teacher to teach.

♣

In nurturing Christians, teaching and learning is the common activity of giving and receiving raised to intentionality, conducted with sensitivity, and completed by an action in kind.

It is like that because Christian experience is.

II. NURTURING ✣ ✣

1. Source

In nurturing Christians, the sources are definitive. Teaching and learning the source of religious experience is the responsive action of knowing and re-enacting.

Some Christians might prefer the singular title, "The Source." Scholars might insist on "Records of The Sources." In either case, what is meant is The Bible, The Judeo-Christian Tradition: sacred history.

And, in any case, there is no question whether this

ON NURTURING CHRISTIANS

history is to be taught: there is only the question how it may be best taught and learned. For nurturing, it is a given.

⚜

In general, the public schools have not been very successful at teaching history. History may well be one of the most disliked subjects in the average high school curriculum. It often appears that the disfavor is profound.

Most history textbooks are dull as dishwater. It is remarkable that after forcible exposure to them anyone ever reads voluntarily again. A recent president of the American Historical Association spoke of the "anti-history animus" of American teachers and attributed it, in part, to the way history is written: "bland, banal or Philistine," he said; "morally obtuse, ethically archaic, intellectually insipid," he continued; "libraries of unreadable books," he concluded.

Further, most Americans are future-oriented. They flaunt a high disregard of the past. The future brought them to these shores, broke the sod of the prairies, and conquered the Far West. Americans have specialized in shaping the future and disregarding the past. John Dewey fixed that indigenous forward tilt on American schools a half-century ago; the only meaning he was willing to assign to the word "god" was that connection between the present and

NURTURING

the future which brings ideals into actuality. Even now, when the frontiers have long been filled, it is vaguely un-American to be satisfied. Industry builds obsolescence so successfully that "newer," "farther," "quicker," and "faster" are still the basic watchwords. This is not the native ground of enthusiasm for history as a schoolroom discipline.

It may even be that mass communication has altered a generation's consciousness of time. When everything happens instantly and there are more current events than one can keep track of, something happens to perspective. In music circles, an "oldie" is a record that was popular eighteen months ago. The early 60s are spoken of by high schoolers as "the olden days." "When were you born?" a teen-ager asked his mother. "'18,'" she replied. "Eighteen hundred and what?" he asked. In San Francisco, a psychedelic poster artist responded to a newspaper interviewer: "You ask funny questions. You still talk to us the same way as like last year you know, but we're not talking the same. There's a gap between us." A brilliantly argued doctoral paper seems to assume that history began with the War: not WWI, but WWII.

Nevertheless, there is a yearning—perhaps no larger than a man's nostalgia—among the young for the old. They adopt the manners and clothing, hair-styles and life-styles, not of their parents, but of their parents' parents. "To decline to look into the Mirror of Then," writes one of their radical heroes, Eldridge

Cleaver, "is to refuse to view the face of Now." They seem to understand that the frontier dream of infinite growth is anachronistic in an age that knows its environment is finite. Some of them seem to grasp that what was wrong with history is that it was presented to them in a linear and secular fashion when they have just discovered that life is multilinear and sacred. Thus, when they are drawn, despite their prejudices, to reading history, as sometimes happens, they almost always read it outside of class and without instruction and they usually read not textbooks but people.

All this provides the context in which the Christian educator deals with history, but it does not form his content or shape his teaching. It is about time to get something stirring in teaching history; if the secular educators can't do it, perhaps the religious educators must. The religious educator's interest in history is not merely to discover how to avoid the catastrophe of repeating mistakes; it is in learning how God acts among men. So he has his own thing to do: exploring human experiences with God in order to generate experiences with God.

⚜

For the Christian, history is personal because it is the recorded result of the living enrichment of personhood. It is personal because it recounts and sustains the divine-human dialogue which constitutes personality in the individual.

NURTURING

For the teacher of Christian history, the content of teaching is formed in the biblical material. It is composed of a series of interlocking occasions on which a person who lived in this place at this time and carried this name did something which illustrates the divine-human interaction in life. Some of the material is factual and some is mythical—which is to say, more than factual. A large part of it is made up of stories about people with peculiarities, strengths, and weaknesses that render them especially credible and interesting. Its content is action rather than conversation. Deeds rather than words are the stuff of the biblical view of life. There are funny stories and sad stories. There are epics and episodes, military yarns and domestic tales, stories of frontier life and of royal courts. People sing and weep, dance and fight, worship and work. All this they do in a small and wasty wilderness where crops come hard and the sun and wind command respect. The hills spoke of eternity and the sea of life, and the people, with tribal jealousies and quarrels, not only could but somehow would illustrate the solidarity of all human saints and sinners. History, in its zigzag course onward, tends toward creation.

And then at last, after innumerable occasions had not been quite ready, there was Jeshua ben Joseph, born during the reign of Herod as King of Judea, who grew up in a northern village and as a young man broke upon the people proclaiming a New Law of Love fulfilling and completing the old laws of the desert and the exile. Rejected by the teachers of the Old Laws, he was accused of treason but convicted for blasphemy, led to "The Place of the Skull," executed, and buried nearby. Three days later he was not in the tomb. His followers said he was alive. They said that he was not lost to them by dying. Before long they affirmed that he had died that man might be restored to God, that God might be made real and knowable to men, that the gulf between God and man had been bridged. The past no longer held men in bondage; the future need no longer hold them in fear. Both had been conquered by the only one who could transcend them, God himself acting as a man among men. They continued to say so for nineteen successive centuries, believing and disagreeing, living and dying, organizing and reforming—people who understood themselves to be his followers and agents. Human life is real because it is experienced to be, and meaningful because God participates in it and gives it new boosts in new and unexpected directions. Thus the events of history add up to a whole greater than the sum of its elements; it is a body of material so clearly embodying the intent of God for man that God mysteriously speaks through it.

For the nurturer of Christians, this content shapes teaching. The purpose of keeping that history green is to precipitate its continuation. Teaching history is the quest for the divine-human dialogue that continuously creates history. It requires learning to stand in events known to be God-infested in such fashion

NURTURING

as to help learners discover God at work everywhere. Because the biblical material made its points in experiential stories rather than in logical syllogisms, the teacher will too. The biblical people sang and danced, wept and worshiped and worked: his classes will sing and dance, weep, worship, and work. History builds spiritual convictions from a complex mosaic of interrelated impressions: the teacher will be content to let the network of ancient and contemporary experiences build its own convictions. If this sort of teaching represents a radical departure from the traditional Bible class, he may remember that the experience-world of the Bible is much more akin to the multilinear one children are now living in than the one which he inherited from his Sunday school teachers.

If classes in the sources of life are linear and dullsville, they are not religion classes. Religion is the discovery of personhood. History is a means to that end.

✣

The teacher of Christianity is the giver of historical knowledge of religion. "To know" in the Bible is an active and personal verb: it means "to be with." Religion is an experience: the discovery that personhood is created by man and God in interaction with the world. Giving is a mutual act: the gift is offered in such fashion that it can be received and given again.

As such a giver, the teacher assumes responsibility for handling the gift.

ON NURTURING CHRISTIANS

He is responsible for accuracy. The teacher's care about handling the gift well enhances the value of the gift. There is a tendency today, especially among the older generation, not to be careful about historical detail. It is probably an inevitable fallout from the knowledge explosion: there is too much to know, so if the general idea is OK, why bother with accuracy. Sloppiness unquestionably devalues.

There are differences, however, between facts. Some are objective, have nothing to do with one's feelings about them, and are the same for everybody and therefore impersonal. They are sometimes called "hard." They will not bend. They do not go away. They are fixed beyond question or doubt. They have to do with dates, places, distances, names. One either has them right or he is wrong. About such facts there is no excuse for inaccuracy. The teacher of Christianity will care about them and get them right.

Not all facts, however, are hard. Some are less objective. They are sometimes called "soft." Some of them are soft because they have not been objectively determined: there is still uncertainty or conflicting data about the date, the place, the distance, or the name. As more information becomes available through research they may become hard. In the field of ancient history one of the more dramatic ways of turning soft into hard facts is archaeology: the actual facts are literally "unearthed." The process may work in reverse, of course, throwing doubt on what had been objective facts. Some facts are soft because their

NURTURING

meaning is not clear: scholarly debates rage about interpretation and significance and with these facts too, the hardness may change from time to time. A teacher needs to keep track of the transitions back and forth between hard and soft facts of this sort. It is a fascinating search, and it goes on all the time. If he cannot enjoy it and share its fascination with his learners, he should not be teaching history.

Other facts are soft because their nature defies objective determination: they have to do with the experiences and interpretations of living. They are nonetheless facts, however, and are knowable through the fundamental commonality of human experiences: since our bodies are alike and we all share sensations and emotions, we can know with direct and subjective certainty how it felt to be somewhere we have never actually been and to experience something we have never actually undergone.

Now, the history of religious experiences occurs in a grid of hard facts, but it consists of soft facts, especially the human, experiential kind. The teacher of Christianity specializes in handling these well; most public school teachers specialize in handling hard facts.

The teacher of religion therefore prefers to deal with the primary sources. Secondary sources help set up the historical grid of hard facts. But he will seldom be satisfied with the so-called curriculum materials distributed by church headquarters because they are seldom accurate enough and almost never provide direct experience with events and people. For the communication of the experience, there is no substitute for meeting the person himself. His ancient source is the Bible. After the biblical period, he will immerse himself in personal revelation: eyewitness account, autobiography, letters, prayers, sermons. He will know the ancient persons at whatever level he is capable of, if not in their own languages then in the best translations and finally in his own paraphrases.

The teacher is also responsible for selectivity. Every detail is important because it is part of the total mosaic of human struggling, stumbling, strutting, serving, suffering, surviving. Every sinner and misfit, though most of them are now nameless and forgotten, is as important to the picture as the saints and kings, whose stories are amply documented. But he cannot even give all of what is known. And he cannot give it all at once. Each class session, therefore, the teacher must choose the parts he offers. He does his best to choose in light of objective criteria, accuracy, and the whole outline, for example. But even so, there is too much, and the choice is ultimately personal. And that is just as it should be. He selects for meaning. And he bears the responsibility for his choice in his own person. The older his students, the more he must be willing to defend his choices; the younger do not know enough yet to challenge. In either case the dynamic is the same: he carries the gift of experience in his own hands. He must be willing for

NURTURING

it to bear his fingerprints. It is the only way religion is nurtured.

The teacher is responsible for the effectiveness of his gift. It is not his responsibility to make the distant near. It is not even his task to make the ancient relevant. His only responsibility is to let it be real. And it may very well be that the harder he tries to make it near and relevant, the more he will obscure its reality. The effective nurturer hands on a history shaped by his own loving handling and bearing the marks of his familiarity. The greatest violence that can be done to history understood to be living encounter is that the teacher give the impression that it is not so.

⚜

To learn history and the Bible as we usually teach them requires skills no child and few adolescents have. Led by educators in the field of history, we have been presenting history in a rigidly linear fashion.

It is said that the learner must master the principle of before-and-after before he can learn history. To achieve this understanding, even in the most empirical matters, he apparently needs to undergo years of vegetables-before-dessert, nap-before-play, study-before-television, saving-before-buying, and so on. It is also said that before he can understand history he must understand how number sequences relate to the dates of the calendar. The year 500 is after the year 450 except, of course, when these years are B.C., in which case 500 is before 450. And except, of course, that much more of importance happened between A.D. 450 and 500 than between 500 and 450 B.C. Teachers in graduate theological seminaries are regularly dismayed to discover that their students have not yet mastered the principle.

Learners of history, it has been assumed, must also grasp the principle of length-of-time. It is related to before-and-after, except that before one can understand history one must be able to grasp the meaning of a century. How does one do that? How long *is* a hundred years? It takes a child years to understand the duration of a day, a lifetime to grasp the length of a year, and as the decades of experience pile up even that understanding changes. A century, therefore, when projected linearly, becomes an abstraction to be grasped intellectually. History is ordinarily conceived and taught, from the very first, in centuries. To "know history" one must be able to *think* "The XIVth Century," and the XIXth and the IVth.

It has also been assumed that the principle of cause-and-effect is essential to learning history. It is modeled on the principle as understood in physics: for every cause there is an appropriate result. The forces of mass and motion provide a convenient example, as, say, on a billiard table. There are many variables, but, with sufficient information, the cause of the cue ball and the effect on the target ball may be calculated. Some have learned, after all, to do it with astounding accuracy. In history, the variables

NURTURING

are even more complex and schools of historical interpretation contend about the application of the principle, but learners must be sufficiently sophisticated to have some understanding of how sequences of events are shaped and limited by their causes.

Now, having along the line got from somewhere some grasp of before-and-after, length-of-time, and cause-and-effect, and having mentally arranged events on a grid of dates and sequences, the average American student is presumably prepared to undertake the great feat of crossing over into another period of time. Few ever accomplish it. Those who do become the great historians. They are usually specialists in a very precise period. They tend to work in libraries and to teach in ivory towers.

This is the way the Bible is taught in seminaries in Europe and the United States and therefore the way it is taught in the schools of what were once called The Mission Fields. Students learned English, or the Western language of their Missionaries, so that they could learn Western subjects like mathematics, physics, and philosophy; so that they could learn the linear concepts of before-and-after, length-of-time, and cause-and-effect; so that they could master Western biblical scholarship; so that they could work their way through the Middle Ages, the fall of Rome, the Byzantine Church, the Church Fathers and the Apologists; so that they could approach the life and thought of Jesus; so that they could understand the world out of which he came.

ON NURTURING CHRISTIANS

It was in a curriculum study of a seminary in the Philippine Islands, and chiefly through the help of the Filipino faculty and students, that it became clear to me that this was not only a long and discouraging journey but that it was also a detour. The rural culture in which they grew up was cognate to the ancient Hebrew. They, too, lived *in* nature—on the earth and in the wind, dampened by the rain and warmed by the sun, dependent on crops which they tended and reaped—and it was alive with transhuman reality. Their dialect, too, was action language. Their history and mythology also were preserved by stories. Their understanding of life was relational. Their logic was nonlinear. Their religion was experiential.

The route for them into the experiential source of the Christian religion could have been—should have been—short and relatively simple. Having made contact with it, their task was to build Christian cultus and theology directly on it. Saved from the necessity of everyone doing the whole task backward, they would be freed to create indigenously, guided by those who could walk the long road and share their knowledge of the dead-end experiments and wrong turnings of other eras in the Western development of Christian forms.

As a book, the Bible is spectacularly adult, challenging the best linear—scholarly—understanding. There should be no evasion of this work. As a record of religious experience, however, the Bible is indige-

NURTURING

nously human. At that level it may be more directly available to today's children's experience than to today's adults'.

✣

The Bible is not so much a book about ancient religion as the source of present religious experience. Therefore, the strategy of teaching it is not so much to get the book into the pupil as to offer the pupil an opportunity to get into it. Adults formed in the old-fashioned, content-centered approach to the Bible tend to think of the world of the Bible as a foreign world. That cannot be true if religious experience is regarded as a fundament of human existence, the Bible as its source book. Teachers formed in traditional methods of instruction tend to think of the Bible as a difficult book to teach. One can find it so only if he approaches it as a material to be mastered from the first by the linear intellectual tools of Western historiography. In that case, the study of the Bible must be begun only in late adolescence or adulthood. However, if the cognate experiences of developing childhood become the contact with it, crossing over into biblical experience may be a much more natural thing than most teachers had ever imagined. They may make it more convincing by themselves crossing over into their pupil's experience of the world.

In the world of the child, experiencing always

comes before conceptualizing. The capacity to experience things like oneself comes before the ability to experience things unlike oneself. The capacity to experience things near at hand comes before the ability to experience things farther removed. The capacity to experience things inside oneself is built upon developing the ability to deal with things outside oneself. Thinking follows handling. Concepts are formed on physical objects. Organizing things is built on the ability to recognize things. Interpretative thinking follows organizing thinking. Interrelational experience is foundational; separation and linearity are learned.

All of these are crossing-experiences—from one location to another, from one mode to another. Crossing into the world of the Bible should not be delayed to be built upon interpretation, coming at the end as a final and difficult accomplishment. It should be done as all learning is done, one step at a time (walking before running), each important for itself (running before hopping), each comfortably completed but leading imperceptibly to the next (hopping before skipping) and each supported by one who has been there before and willing to come back and do it again for the sake of the learner.

In the field of developmental experience, generalizations must never be grasped tightly. They are guidelines only. The pace of each child will differ. Each group of children will differ. An effective nurturer knows the generalizations and the children.

NURTURING

✣

AGES FOUR AND FIVE: *Stories from the biblical material told for their human interest alone.*

To use the Bible in this way will be to use it in its own way. Its language is composed of events and actions rather than of words and ideas. Hebrew sentences usually begin with the verb. The Hebrew word *amar* means both thought and speech: "thinking aloud." The Hebrew thinks "with the senses"—the whole body. Everything is concrete and definite, and he leaps from this experience directly to intuitive conclusions, skipping almost always the steps of abstraction and testing. Stories embody this thought-world.

What is to be shared between the child and the ancient experience is the pure joy of person-and-event. Let there be no moralizing, no contemporizing, no interpretation, no memorizing, no dates, no adult piety to obscure that joy. It is all mythic to them, that is to say, more than mere life. Gay stories, sad stories, wonder stories, love stories, battle stories—all in riotous mixture. Let the stories be told in the child's language, and let it be clearly understood that this means abandoning the adult Elizabethan vocabulary of the King James Version. It also means paraphrasing freely and eloquently. The premium now is not on historical accuracy (what does the pre-school child know or care of that?) but on modal accuracy, the simple verb-and-noun liveliness of happenings and human behavior. Tell them around the campfire as the Hebrews did before they wrote them down: at least in a group on the floor with questions and interruptions forming and shaping the story-event. Find the best storytellers in the community and simply turn them loose with the Bible and the children. Week after week! Over and over, with an imaginative injection of biblical stories they haven't heard yet, suggested by pure verbal and emotional association rather than by adult notions of historical sequence.

The goal is a direct and easy relation to an ancient people who do not seem to be strangers. The fundamental mosaic of meaning is building, and the basic religious experience of crossing over has begun.

AGES SIX AND SEVEN: *Stories presented from the primary source.*

This means reading aloud from the book. All the purposes and qualities of telling are to be preserved. So the stories must be read as skillfully and freely as talent and training can permit. *As stories,* still. Find the best readers in town. No stumbling on names. No intoning. No mock piety. But living people and their actions coming off the page through the living person of the reader and directly to the living experience of the hearer. Let the reader find the translations that work best for him and for his listeners. As familiarity increases, he may find the children interested in the King James Version. Let the reader discover the sequences of stories that hold the children's interest. As the sequences enlarge, he may find himself read-

NURTURING

ing whole epics. Let the reader give the children a chance to hear songs and psalms as they relate to the moods of the stories. And let him be as free as he and the children wish in conversation about the material: as the attention span of the group grows, this will tend to come after the story rather than during it. Let the conversation be led by the children; as they become familiar with the material, their questions may become probing beyond anticipation. And imperceptibly the group will move toward the next phase as their capacity develops: they have already been readying for the crossover into enactment. Then let the reader surrender the group to another leader and turn himself to a coming group of six-year-olds ready to hear the Bible read as only he can.

AGES EIGHT TO TWELVE: *re-enactment.*

This phase will probably begin with simple movement in response to the rhythms and sounds of the material. As the material becomes familiar the improvisation may be simultaneous with the words. Eventually, the children will indicate that they want to "play" the story themselves. The reader becomes a prompter, supplying speeches and reminders of action when needed. The discussion at the conclusion will eventually turn to accuracy. The learning of before-and-after has begun, not as a logical concept but as a childlike way of seeing the relation between things. When the conversation turns to interpretation, the learning of cause-and-effect is already under way.

ON NURTURING CHRISTIANS

Most of two years of this period can be devoted to the fundamental and enormously significant task of physically crossing over into the biblical world. It is a world in which most children of this age are instinctively interested: it came from the childhood of the race and it is concerned with the earth, the trees, and the sky, and how to make a life with them as his companions. It is a lively world inviting him to participation and a vasty world challenging him to penetration. He is beginning to possess the skills of body and mind to understand it by coping with it. As, need it be said, the Hebrews and Israelites did. Crossing over into it from his familiar but unnatural world of cement, electric gadgets, plumbing, and synthetic fabrics may be one of the most meaningful experiences of his life.

Let the children have the Bedouin experience, as deeply and as realistically as may be. No more miniature Palestinian villages of milk cartons and salt-and-flour paste on *papier-mâché* hillsides on a table top in the corner of the classroom. Rather, let them—as families, and that means with adult help, of course, but not quite as teachers—construct a Palestinian house and courtyard. They were not large—perhaps six by eight feet and less than six feet high. They were not difficult to build—poles set in the ground with roof beams lashed across flat, interwoven with smaller branches and daubed with mud, or built from the ground up with sundried earthen bricks. A doorway. An opening or two for windows, perhaps. The

NURTURING

ground was the floor. Outside there was a bee-hive adobe-brick oven in which food was cooked and on top of which the earthen pottery was fired. The pottery was made of the damp clay of stream beds and formed by hand. The bread was made of the grain they grew, hand ground, and mixed into yeastless dough rolled out on a stone and baked on another. The garments were straight pieces of handspun goat-hair material woven on looms made of sticks. The colors were from dyeing in the juices of berries and roots in the hand-turned home-fired pots. The family slept together on the earth floor of their one-room house, and except when the weather drove them in they lived outside.

In the process of a class entering this indigenous world let the spirit and mind of the God-intoxicated people soak in through the pores of their skin and become part of them. Let them reconstruct the Hebrew festivals. Let them become familiar with the psalms. Let them hear the prophecies in context. Let them participate in the life and wisdom of Jesus. The Bible need never again be a foreign world to them nor its religious experience an alien one. The sense of historical cause-and-effect is coming into focus through their bones.

AGES THIRTEEN TO FIFTEEN: *facts*.

Facts galore have been dealt with existentially in the reliving of biblical life. The time to isolate and

ON NURTURING CHRISTIANS

organize them comes next, and the need to do so will be signaled in dozens of ways.

First, the hard facts: dates, names, people, places, distances. Thirteen is the time of fascination with information: batting averages, George Washington's wooden false teeth, the displacement of automobile engines, the middle names of Vice Presidents, the capitals of obscure countries. It will apply itself to the biblical material as well. If the answer is there, look it up; if it is not, run it down in secondary sources. No offhand opinions or generalizations will do. Have a teacher who can honestly treat the passion for unrelated items of data with respect and has the patience to find and verify them.

Now is the time for maps. Ancient Jerusalem, Palestine, the Fertile Crescent. Let them be large, covering an entire wall or floor or parking lot. Let them be in relief. And let them be accurate to the fraction of the scale.

Then outlines. Isolated sequences, periods, and phases and their relationships. First in limited compass, then more and more extensive and integrated. Now is the time, not as it is so often done by well-meaning history teachers in the first and second grades, to produce the Time-Line. Let it be enormous, large enough in scale to get in details of people, events, and reigns; let it be long enough to get it all in. Let it be illustrated with pictures and artifacts and aphorisms. It may go all the way around the room, down the hall, across a play area. The prin-

NURTURING

ciple of before-and-after is shaping up, and the duration-of-time is taking on spatial meaning.

And finally, as the hard facts are organized, the soft facts come into view. Not everything can be dated and placed with certainty. But then comes the realization that they have been experienced in the re-enacting stage already. When it is recognized that these may be the more important facts, history has come alive. So there should be a period of time, perhaps a year, devoted to recognizing and sorting them: feelings, commitments, wisdom—treated as facts but not confused with hard facts. The prophets can fall into place among the kings and battles, the intertestamental period in the context of Greece, Jesus and his interpreters in the setting of Rome. The duration-of-time has begun to have meaning—time occupied with living, thinking, and suffering; duration established by personal residence.

AGES SIXTEEN TO EIGHTEEN: *interpretation.*

This is the time for thought and talk.

Given any kind of background and some support, the middle adolescent turns naturally to philosophy. Deprived of the background, he tends to become withdrawn and secretive; given any kind of resistance, he becomes fiercely philosophical. Now he needs an adult at hand who knows the biblical source and loves to argue. Endlessly. Who is not distressed by the wildest speculations because he knows in his bones that abstract thought is a newfound skill and needs to be enormously exercised. As with muscle skills, only practice makes as perfect as can be. Who can patiently recall the hard facts and the outlines and the soft facts. Who can tie them as tethers into adolescent flights of fancy. Around and around they'll go. A carrousel is always more interesting for the ride than for the scenery.

First, the practical interpretations: ethics, morality, personal values. Adolescents are all idealists at heart. But their world isn't. So were the people of the Christian source, and neither was their world. The sessions will not be structured in the ordinary classroom sense; sessions will be structured by the learners' needs.

Then, the literary interpretations: a time will come when adolescents will be interested in an analysis of their source, and then they will need a skilled and informed teacher to lead them. If the interest is precipitated by a course in school, their religious teacher needs to be as competent a literary critic as they will meet there. In any case, he needs to be the best the church can offer. The questions of authorship, historicity, and style are often important ones at this period. Teachers and learners must honestly dig into the form of the message, its originality and appropriateness and effectiveness. It can be expected that the entire investigation will be conducted more informally and more profoundly than the same students' study of Shakespeare.

It is likely that the whole group of 16, 17, and

NURTURING

18-year-olds will not move together in their interests. Therefore it is advisable to be able to offer courses such as those described above in relatively small segments, letting the learners develop their own pace and interests. If possible, a repeated series of electives would provide the needed freedom of interest.

ADULTHOOD: *philosophical interpretation.*

The quest of the source of religious experience is a need that is never finally filled in human life. It is true that a great desuetude regarding religion usually sets in during early adulthood, but that is the unnatural result of conditioning by irrelevant and boring teaching of history. A great deal of makeup work may be required of many adults. It may be necessary to establish the missed experiences of childhood and adolescence. One of the best ways to accomplish that is to interest them in learners and help them to become good teachers. Returning to childhood and adolescence through the experience of present-day children and adolescents is a thoroughly respectable and effective way to fill in one's own gaps. And especially if they are teachers, it is essential that the adult quest continue constantly. Only the active learner can be a good teacher.

In adulthood, the earlier sequence of practical then abstract thinking is usually reversed. The young adult ordinarily is passionate for the theoretical and abstract. The older adult ordinarily is much more interested in practical applications. In any case, the

ON NURTURING CHRISTIANS

purpose is the building of a working philosophy of sacred history, a task in pursuit of which the power of the relationship between God and man is released again and again. If the task is to be participating in history, biblical courses as near the graduate seminary level as is possible are to be expected. Every community of learning needs a resident biblical scholar. Every biblical scholar needs a community of learning. Let them find ways to produce each other.

♣

For nurturing Christians, teaching and learning sacred history consist in re-enacting, at the profoundest dimensions possible, the spiritual experiences which precipitated it. It means participating in God's acts among people. If history is taught differently from most teaching of history, it is because the Christian teacher understands both history and teaching differently.

2. Scene

In nurturing Christians, the scene is community. Teaching and learning community is the responsive action of inviting and participating.

Some Christians will prefer the formal title, "The Church." Scholars might insist on the early Christian word "Koinonia." In either case, what is meant is responsive interaction of the individual person with other persons, the world, and God.

In any case, teaching and learning Christianity takes place in relation. Christian experience is an interaction between the individual and God. It is not unlike the interaction between human persons. So far as is known, it never takes place apart from the individ-

ON NURTURING CHRISTIANS

ual's relation to persons. But the Christian interest in community is not merely to prevent loneliness: it is to certify the divine-human relation. Therefore, the nurturing community of Christianity is more than a human huddling. It is a gathering of people who care. They care about one another. It is sometimes called "brotherhood." They also care about those who do not care for them. Therefore the caring is sometimes called "vicarious." They also care for things. So it is also sometimes called "sacramental." They care about God. That caring is sometimes called "worship." Together all this inter-caring may be called "love."

♣

It sometimes appears that the organized church has not done very well at nurturing love. Cynics like to point in scorn to the persecution of heretics and the pursuit of holy wars. Other cynics like to point to the irrelevance of the church on the corner to the issues of society. These are clearly perversions of community and are caused by caring too much about one of the constituent relations of love to the exclusion of others. Linearity is always artificial and destructive in a relationship that is fundamentally multi-linear.

Love and community are not easy to come by anywhere these days, in spite of the frequent quotation of John Donne's dictum that "no man is an island." It would appear that Western society has been mak-

NURTURING

ing toward this end for some time. The outline is familiar and has been theorized variantly.

The Middle Ages was a vast period, producing many diverse forms of life, but characterized by a profound unity. "The great gray face" of the Middle Ages is an oversimplification, but life was relatively alike and dull for the vast majority and organized into unity by the feudal and ecclesiastical systems as well as formed into unity by superstition and religious faith. There was undoubtedly as much intimate relationship as in any society, but love was defined as vertical and ontological. Unity was established by God's unilateral being and maintained by the church's hierarchical authority.

In the 16th and 17th centuries the movements called Renaissance and Reformation initiated separation between church and culture and the freedom of the individual. The Renaissance meant release from the otherworldliness and self-denial of the Medieval period, and a devotion to self-realization and the pursuit of individuality in manners, dress, and belief. The Reformation emphasized the individual's responsibility directly to God alone, but held individualism in check momentarily by a strong emphasis on the fellowship of worship and faith.

The 17th and 18th centuries were marked by the extensions of reason and an almost unbelievable ecstasy in the discovery of this human power. The individuality of mind spurred style, elegance, and form. But there was also a huge, ignored, and un-

ON NURTURING CHRISTIANS

reasonable lower class, and the period ended with a burst of individualism from below creating a series of spectacular political revolutions in favor of "the common man."

The 19th century turned the powers of individual minds to solving the preliminary problems of science, exploring geographical frontiers, and creating massive individual as well as national empires. The American scene, with its frontier to be conquered, Civil War to be equipped and fought, and fortunes to be made, developed a special kind of individualism. Personal rights were established on individual heroism, and every man claimed his own reward for pluck and determination. It was a man against the world.

In the 20th century, the methods of science and industry have taken over the scene to produce what has been called "the technocratic man." Everything, from scientific knowledge to household gadgetry, seems to have added to the compartmentalization of life. Knowledge is departmentalized. Specialists are segregated. Society is ghettoized. Education is systematized. Families are isolated. Children are stratified. In general, persons are depersonalized by the changes in history, and there is great despair about love and community.

Speaking for many natives of the contemporary world, James Baldwin describes his Harlem youth in a universe "which has made no terms for your existence, has made no room for you." "I'm afraid I'm going to get a system instead of a life," cries the

NURTURING

agonized undergraduate trying to reach his adviser to make a change in his key-punched class card. "I was managed through a grade school, a high school, and now a college system." Erich Fromm calls love "a marginal phenomenon" in present-day society. By his analysis we are automatons, having been made so by a capitalist society. Prevented from becoming persons, he suggests, we have become packages. Charles Reich argues in *The Greening of America* that men no longer run the machines they have invented but merely tend them, and he warns that "the machine is beginning to destroy itself." "There is only one way to a life of love," according to the infamous Revolutionary Force 9 in New York City, "to attack and destroy." We all know how the appearance of human relations is provided by staying close to the herd, not being noticeably different in thought, feeling, or action. While striving for geographical proximity in cities and suburbs, co-ed dormitories and sensitivity groups, everybody remains alone. Krishnamurti, in one of his more Oriental moments, warns today's young people against looking for love in relationships: "it is in you," he says; and when looking in yourself for love, don't look for love, he warns—"look for the hurt when someone ignores you." In desperation, Marcuse joins Fromm in arguing that love has been prevented by society and that the only remedy now is for naturally loving mankind to reach unilaterally into the society he has created to end division of labor and discrimination of property so

ON NURTURING CHRISTIANS

that society may be completely eroticized, love flowing equally toward everybody everywhere.

✣

During the 20s and 30s, religious education made a brief but brilliant attempt to socialize both religion and education. The movement was called "progressive religious education," and the prophet was George Albert Coe who taught at Union Theological Seminary and stated the core of his approach in *A Social Theory of Religious Education*. "Indwelling love" is Coe's first principle of learning, and education for Coe consists of providing for children "conditions in which love is experienced" so consistently and consciously that it will progressively become both habit and faith.

The first step is to make pupils acquainted with persons who really love them. The process begins in the home. In the school the disciplined adult love of the teachers becomes the support and catalyst for the children's love for one another. Day by day the class is led to become a sharing group, by its own internal relations becoming a little "beloved community." Rules and regulations and schedules are to be discarded as obstructions to this learning process.

The second phase is more difficult: the enlargement of this first experience of group life to larger and more extended groups. The interpersonal relationships begun in the family are opened out to the

NURTURING

world in steps as large and rapid as the individuals and groups can take: church, community, races, classes, nation, world. The goal is that the whole world become "a society of persons." That goal is reached by education, "an expanding series of social relations," consciously undertaken and directed in love.

A great deal of actual learning and experimental discovery are involved in turning negative relationships into positive ones throughout life. Also in the process, the learner discovers God. There was no doubt in Coe's mind that the human capacity to practice and enlarge love had to do with God. It was not, however, merely bestowed upon man by God. God is a personality-seeking inclination in the world's life and realizes himself by promoting personality-realization everywhere. Thus it is through "some human godlikeness" that human beings know God. They are most likely to discover it by cooperating with God in his drive to achieve a society in which love operates, in which "there is no separation between human society and divine." In his fusion of divine love with human love, Jesus made it clear that the ideal society is a democratic and participatory divine-human community.

Person-oriented, religion-motivated education of this sort following World War I became definitive among liberal Protestants and influential even among conservatives. Its emphases on experiencing love and learning community are indispensable. During the calamitous 30s and 40s, the worldwide breakdown of community shook the foundations of human self-confidence, and it became clear that humanity could not save itself by merely enlarging its aggregations. Now, in the post–WWII period, we are regaining some confidence in the power of being-together. For whatever reasons, the religious community has been slower than some parts of the secular community to regain its shattered image of self-productivity. Secular encounter and sensitivity groups, symbolized perhaps by Essalen in its romantic setting near Big Sur, have taken the initiative in finding salvation in relation. George Leonard has brilliantly secularized Coe's religious education in his much-discussed *Education and Ecstasy*.

However, Coe had the right scene for nurturing Christians: 'the ultimate relation," he called it, "in which God, the child and the adult . . . stand to each other." His error, induced by the self-sufficiency of his time, was to suppose that this multidimensional relationship could be made linear—from home to the world—and unilateral—from man to God—by a straight-line educational process. The scene of Christian nurture is like its source, a dynamic interaction among persons and the divine in time and the world.

⚜

It is clear by now that this sort of community never comes easy and that attempts to simplify it are

NURTURING

disastrous. The nature of anything is defined by its most refined and fulsome example rather than by its simplest and earliest. In the Judeo-Christian tradition, the Garden of Eden is the mythical archetype of community and in it were contained the essential ingredients: individual persons in love, things, God. It was, however, as yet untested by history. It cannot, therefore, be taken as the model. The definition of community is derived from the Kingdom (or city or world) of God. It is presently a vision which is yet to come into actuality through history.

Between definition and actuality there is a great deal of ground to be covered and many lessons to be learned. Community is not merely the product of genial group grope. The Hebraic community was built through two thousand years of divine-human interaction. A people was formed in history from what had been a no-people. Within a weak and oppressed minority in an ancient empire, power appeared. To Israel it was the love of Yahweh, who delivered her from the house of bondage, gave her the land of milk and honey, and in doing so had shown his power over the forces of nature, Pharaoh, and the armies of Canaan. However, leaving Egypt a nothing-people they had centuries to go before they became Yahweh-people. They made many mistakes in judgment, they followed many wrong trails, fought many wrong enemies, and struggled into the Promised Land. There they pledged allegiance to wrong gods, insisted on wrong kinds of government, followed their own wicked kings, and made treaties with the wrong foreign kings. Carried off into Exile, they tilled wrong soils, built wrong cities, worshiped in wrong temples, and struggled back into purity and unity. And finally they saw that Yahweh punishes those whom he loves and that together they create a community of love-on-earth.

The Christian community was built on a new law of love. It may be practiced now, though everything is neither perfect nor easy yet. "You have heard it said that you should love your neighbors and hate your enemies," he said; "I say to you, love your enemies, bless them that curse you, do good to them that hate you." The community is where that law of love is lived. "My kingdom," he said, "is not of this world"; "it is not merely there or here"; "it is in and among you."

So the leaders of established communities of other sorts rejected him and eventually executed him. So love is God's thorny path to humanity. It is a free gift, creative of free response in kind; it makes possible "a life more abundant" than mere survival. It is an unselfish love "which seeks not its own." It can give and expend itself prodigiously because it is reproductive, not in essence but in action. So there is in turn the early Christian community and its understanding of love. Love treats persons and sometimes things as if they were living beings. It seeks to possess the beloved in order to give it life. In passion it reaches out to embrace its subject; in reason it seeks

NURTURING

to identify it with oneself. In seeks to produce, in reason as well as in passion, others similar to oneself. It seeks to create response to oneself. It initiates the occasion of loving response. It makes the first move, knowing the risk of rejection. It therefore invites the suffering servant role for itself, and it cannot afford the indulgence of surprise or resentment when suffering and servanthood are assigned. It is practiced as well as possible because the Christian community knows it to be creative of the world.

This definitive sort of community is the scene of Christian nurturing. Past experiences of attempting to live with it suggest strongly that when the historical source is not kept alive and operative the experiment is short-lived. Whether the people are aware of those roots, the community is unified by intended relation to God. It is a group in which people do things because they care about being children of God. One of the things they do is to nurture. It is a community to be experienced in ever-widening and more complex circles. It is also a community centered on effectiveness and depth in limited circles. Nurturing may be understood as doing both of these things simultaneously.

Whether the institutional or local church is such a scene may be a matter of concern to churchmen and of interest to church critics, but it is more or less irrelevant. Christians are not nurtured without it, whatever it is called, and wherever it does exist the Christian experience is taught-and-learned. If it is

ON NURTURING CHRISTIANS

not characteristic of the denominational organization, let it be of the local church; if it is not characteristic of the local church, let it be of the church school; if it is not characteristic of the church school, let it be of the class; if it is not characteristic of every session of the class, let it be of this session. It is possible that churches may be disquieted, but it is the only route to the Kingdom of God.

♣

Community is not something to be taught apart from the source of religious experience as if it were an added curricular element on which educational expertise is to be focused during designated class sessions. In fact, it can probably not be taught at all. It is a shared experience: i.e., it is nurtured rather than taught. By nature (and therefore by definition), shared relationship is the natural setting of religious experience. This sort of thinking comes as no surprise to innumerable and unforgettable Aunt Marthas who have taught the Bible in Sunday school for years because they loved children: what they said about The Book may have been largely forgotten, but their love has not. It will surprise only educators who have supposed that children learn best only when they concentrate unilaterally on one thing at a time and that concentrating assumes that subjective feelings must be eliminated. Love is the natural fundament of child experience; only later does it become a problem, and then it must be dealt with problematically in the light of prior experience.

Thus, in the world of the child as always, experiencing comes before conceptualizing. The capacity to love begins with the experience of being loved. Psychologists and sociologists are pretty well agreed, after considerable scratching about with other theories, on what everybody always knew: the human animal does not survive infancy without love. The child's first communal awareness, therefore, is of a psychic unity sometimes called "we-ness." There is little or no discrimination of individuality. Individuality, "I-ness," begins to develop with the determination of the differences between "self" and "other." That awareness apparently originates in the discovery of "other-ness" in persons, perhaps of father or siblings first, and only then is extrapolated to an awareness of the other-ness of objects. This is a project that takes a long time and perhaps continues throughout life as the objects of experience become more complex and challenging. Some people apparently prefer to live their entire lives dominated by the other-ness of things. Ordinarily, however, other-ness is permeated by a development of "I-ness"; it begins in relation to persons: in childhood, peer-age play-groups and then class-groups; in adolescence, peer-age persons of the same sex and then of the other; throughout life, other-age persons first of the same sex and then of the other, of the same again, and then without regard to sex. Apparently only on the foundation of a healthy I-awareness can a happy and productive network of I-and-other relationships be built and regulated.

All of these are community-building, love-expanding experiences: the scene of Christian nurturing. It is the setting in which the biblical experience is real and operative. Christian experience will be nurtured as these levels of experiencing are lovingly lived through and conceptualized.

In the field of developmental experience, it is good to be reminded that generalizations must never be held too rigidly. They are guidelines only. The pace of each child will differ. Each group of children will differ. An effective nurturer knows both the generalizations and the children.

⚜

AGES FOUR AND FIVE: *getting along together.*

At this level, the scene of Christian nurturing does not look or feel very different from any good nursery school or kindergarten.

Everything is activity. The children are busy with toys, especially those designed to develop the co-ordination of the larger muscles and the sense of order. An adult would say that they "play." But it must be remembered that playing is the most important educational thing that children do. By playing with things they are establishing individual iden-

NURTURING

tity, i.e., working out "I-ness" in relation to "otherness." It is an individual task. Gradually they move to playing with things with one another. From the child's point of view, this involves an enormous extension of the experience of I-and-other. From the psychologist's point of view, they are furthering individual identity by establishing relationships with others—those most like themselves—their peers. From the adult's point of view, the scene is an extension of the home. The teachers are extensions of the parents. The room is an extension of the house at home. It is unlike the home in many ways: there are several parents (aunts and uncles), the house is larger ("our" collective house), there are many more peers (a special "family"). It is often a difficult learning experience, and it needs to be undertaken patiently and lovingly.

AGES SIX AND SEVEN: *trusting an adult (not a parent)*.

In most public schools, children are teacher-worshipers during the first few months of the First Grade; in many they have become either teacher-obeyers or teacher-resisters by the time the Second Grade recesses for the summer. There is a heavy carry-over from the public school classroom to the church school classroom and sometimes into the home. It is important that this development not be characteristic of Christian nurturing. There the task is not initiation into a system but rather the exploration of love-and-community. The primary responsibility of the nurturing Christian is to offer and receive trust. It is not a simple task or a thornless path. Adults betray children without half trying. The adults in this classroom must therefore be hypersensitive to keeping faith, knowing that trust will break down inevitably because of the humanness of everyone involved, but that breakdown may always be the source of buildup. Community is redemptive. Some teachers can work at trust-building directly, others develop it indirectly as the offshoot of doing other things together. In any case, it is the scene of religious experience for these years: teachers (perhaps they should be called something else) are there, trusting and risking, because they care, because they have discovered that God cares. It ought to show.

AGES EIGHT TO TWELVE: *accomplishing things as a group.*

The community establishes and defines itself in relation to physical things. The ideal is a group building project of some sort. It should probably be practical enough so that the group (including the teachers) may enjoy the product themselves. It should be complex enough so that many different kinds and sizes of objects are involved (miniaturization—model-making—is not natural for the younger years of this stage but holds great fascination for many during the later years). It should be extensive enough so that no individual can accomplish it alone (even

NURTURING

the adult leaders). It should extend long enough so that time and continuity become dimensions of its accomplishment. It should be sufficiently defined so that it is accomplishable by the group. This is no time, incidentally, to introduce children to the *deus ex machina* of covert adult rescue from an impossible undertaking: success-and-failure interlocked should be part of the nurturing experience, and neither by itself.

It should be obvious that several projects in some sort of continuum will be required. It may be well to select adult leadership for the group in terms of their project interests and skills, giving them primary responsibility for the duration of the project they can best guide. In any case, the process of learning to be together by working together is the scene: it is undertaken because the children themselves are learning to care.

AGES THIRTEEN TO FIFTEEN: *finding individuality in the group.*

These are the years of grouping and regroupings, usually homosexual and then heterosexual, individual crushes and recoveries, in-groups and out-groups often symbolized by clothing, and constant reshuffling of clicques. Ordinarily the development is asymmetrical between males and females. The girls are usually ready for heterosexual groupings months before the boys. Often all their interests are very different from the boys, clothes and reading and music

ON NURTURING CHRISTIANS

for example as contrasted to sports and motorcycles and camping. Almost always these interests are intense, exclusive, and of short duration. The girl who does not find the predominant preoccupations of her girlfriends to be hers is often very lonely.

Relationally, it is a trying time for everyone. Leaders (adult friends?) will demonstrate that they care for teen-agers best not by attempting to identity with them. Young people sense from experience that there is no relationship without individuality, and they regard attempts by adults to become one of them as surrender of individuality. They will meet the teen-agers better by being flexible. They will advance the teen-agers' painful search for individuality best by being always their own individual selves in the changing patterns of adolescence. They will let the groups form and dissolve, being always fully present as themselves. Enforcing large co-ed groupings of the entire class is the system of the public schools: let the scene of Christian nurturing be more personal and flexible.

Educationally, it is a trying time for everyone, especially if education be defined formally and linearly. Teen-agers talk. They need to talk more than they need to make sense. The adult does not need to share it all. There will also, if only because of the statistical probabilities inherent in huge amounts of verbalization, be occasional flashes of insight and unpredictable moments of thoughtfulness. Let the adult always be present for them, though not necessarily talking during them. Let the adult always sup-

NURTURING

port individuality in the group with his own independence and love. His responsibility is to nurture rather than to teach.

AGES SIXTEEN TO EIGHTEEN: *understanding how things are accomplished in groups.*

Sixteens, seventeens, and eighteens are thinkers. Their communities find and establish themselves in relation to conceptual things. One of the chief reasons for boredom in high school is that teachers do not appear to be thinkers.

The scene of nurturing in this period is thinking together as and about groups. The young people need thinking-projects that will stretch their capacities: theories of how groups work. Their own groups: interpersonal dynamics and how the theories are practiced, why groups break down, what holds them together. Personal groups: dating, marriage, home, communes. Practical groups: organizing to get things done. Political groups: the dynamics of protesting, voting, gaining and exchanging power. Exotic groups: other religions and cultures, what their people do together and why, i.e., ritual and social and ethical practices.

Dealing with all this is "process": the adult leaders need to be adept at knowing where data are to be found (often enough in the town or area itself and from people rather than from books) and to be effective in offering them at moments when they are needed if thinking is to go on smoothly and responibly. The goal at this level, however, is product rather than process. At the lower project level, ages 8-12, the focus could be on process because the material was objective; at this project level, ages 16-18, the emphasis needs to be on an identifiable product because the material tends to be subjective. The leader has the responsibility, therefore, to bring thinking projects to conclusions which can be stated and objectified (probably, life and teen-agers being what they are, to be refined and changed). And somehow, he will make it known that he leads in these ways because he cares.

ADULTHOOD: *coping with change within groups.*

Community continues to be the scene of Christian nurturing. Maintaining continuity tends to be the problem. Adult groups are constantly changing: the family enlarges in size and then diminishes; the relationships of the home become more complex, demanding, challenging, satisfying; work groupings develop, solidify, shift; interest groups change from decade to decade; those who had been members of various groups begin to move away, then pass away. In addition, the pace of social change is increasing in what appears to be geometrical progression: racial, class, economic, and political storms are under way that make waves for everybody. Our era may be likened to the wilderness wandering of the ancient Hebrews after the triumphant Exodus from Egypt.

NURTURING

They found people-hood then, partly perhaps because survival depended on it, but partly also because their precarious situation exposed them to the purposes and love of Yahweh. The mataphor suggests that in a time of social wandering the community of love must be involved, if not influencing the nature of the changes at least standing for the possibility of renewing the covenant of love with divinity. Individuals and communities can survive to serve only by learning to care effectively in groups. The scene of nurturing turns out to be life-wide.

⚜

It may be useful for the Christian community to do something somewhat dramatic and counter-culture as a way of establishing and demonstrating its uniqueness.

Practical programs of community reform often serve that purpose. Christian involvement in the Labor Movement, Women's Rights, Prison Reform, Temperance, Civil Rights, and Peace have, in succession, given substance to the Christian claim to be a community of love.

The strategy may be useful in determining emphases for nurturing. In the public schools, homogenous grouping has become so much a part of the system that it is often thought to define the educational processes. School children are segregated from society into groups of thirty or so all within a year of one another's age. Even these groups are further homogenized by grouping children according to capacity. Children spend two thirds of the first fifth of their waking lives exclusively with others who differ by only a few months and IQ points. Further, they are segregated from the majority of adults in society by their teachers and administrators who control their school lives and exclude parents as outsiders unqualified to criticize or evaluate.

The community of Christian nurturing could easily become an entirely different scene by cutting across all this homogenization and deliberately opening up childhood experience to wider and richer relationships.

Let senior citizens be introduced into children's groups. One may specify the four-and-five and the six-and-seven-year-old classes without excluding the older groups. Children need grandparents: almost universally, culture, history, and values have been communicated to children not by parents but by grandparents. No father can very successfully say, "Let me tell you about when I was your age"; grandparents can always say, "Let me tell you about when your father was a boy," or even more exciting, "about when I was a child." Cultural traditions and values are nurtured at the grandparents' knee. But late 20th-century American society is a world without visible grandparents: the modern family moves frequently and the grandparents are usually "back home," an aged and not always welcome occasional

NURTURING

presence. Even at home senior people are segregated into retirement communities, where they may enjoy life without children underfoot, gardens to keep, and home repairs to make, but invisible to the rest of the workaday world. The question may be how long American culture will last with this crucial hiatus at its heart. By the same token, in every community there are grandparents with no grandchildren of their own at hand. They need each other. The nurturing community could provide them with each other.

Parents need to know other children than their own, and one may specify teen-agers without excluding the other age-groups. Teen-agers need to know other parents than their own. Each needs to find out that the other is human after all. Living always in the relationship of parental authority is very different from being together in voluntary thinking and doing. Let some of the more formal teaching-and-learning be in interest groups cutting across all ages. Let the parents enlarge community by being instructed by someone younger; let young people enlarge community by solving problems with someone older; because they are interested in the same subject matter let them find each other.

Children need to know children different from their own age but near it. Let children who have completed a learning task guide younger ones through it. Both Jesuit and Lutheran schools of the 16th century practiced the principle, and so did the American one-room school of the 19th century. It

ON NURTURING CHRISTIANS

was good theory then, and it should be now. It was effective then, and it may be even more effective now. In a culture booked with fictional anti-heroes and real non-heroes, youngsters need some plain heroes they can see and reach—kids a few years older who will share what they have just learned and what the younger are about to learn—and they need to be ordinary heroes to some kids just younger than they.

In the Junior High age, let the boys and girls be separated but the age-span of the boys' groups and the girls' groups enlarged. Young-teens need to know more than the uncomfortableness of their peers and the authority of their adults. Older-teens need to remember where they just came from.

Someone needs to demonstrate that community is the scene of learning by caring enough about it to do it in distinctive ways.

♣

Nurturing Christians is conducted in a community of loving persons who love God. The reality of God drives them to one another. Relating to one another opens the way to God. It is a covenant which sustains and enriches life.

3. Stance

In nurturing Christians, stance is the position one takes up in life. Teaching and learning stance is the responsive action of offering and building.

Some Christians will prefer to say "beliefs." Religious scholars will most easily say "theology." In either case, what is meant is relating thinking to religious experience.

In teaching and learning Christianity, theology is inescapable. It should characterize the whole process; ordinarily, it is thought to be only a product of the process.

Theology is usually understood to be thinking *about* one's religion. The obvious implication is that religious experience has "occurred," that one's religion has been "formed," and that one can step away from it to look at it, verbalize it, and evaluate it. He is free to use whatever style of thinking comes most easily to him, and in our culture it is usually either scientific or analytic. He will, for example, think about Luther's "Here I stand, I can do no other, God help me." In this case, theology is indeed a product; it is a thing, a system, a conclusion. It is the last item of a linear sequence.

Theology may be better understood, however, as thinking *with* one's religion. Then the attempt will be to think in terms of one's experience of religion. Since religious experience is interrelational and dynamic by nature, theologizing will be the effort to think through everything in multilinear ways. He will try to think religiously, rather than scientifically or analytically. He will, for example, attempt to do what Luther was doing when he said, "Here I stand." In this case, theology is a process and stance is not a head-down obdurance but a figure cut on the way to somewhere.

⚜

Not a great deal is known about teaching theology. The subject is forbidden to the public schools, both lower and higher, so they have no experience or educational theory for religious educators to draw on.

Organized religion has been teaching theology for centuries, of course. In the Christian Movement,

NURTURING

schooling in theology developed very early and schools came soon.

Throughout the 2nd and 3rd centuries and reaching back into the 1st and on into the 4th, the double phenomenon of the persecution of Christians and the spread of Christianity necessitated the careful instruction of new Christians. They were almost all converts from some other religion. They were almost all adults. They needed to know where they stood.

The *catechumenate* was the church's first answer. As the individual passed through stages of increasingly intimate participation in the Christian community, he was instructed in scripture, tradition, and ritual. Much of the instruction was line-by-line memorizing. But memory was reinforced and tested by daily sharing and risk. There was a double result: an incredible courage in stance-taking, and a fixation of authoritative content and interpretation. When the church was recognized and persecution ceased, the latter came to be thought of as theology.

Perhaps the most interesting and influential school of early Christianity was the one that emerged in the university city of Alexandria. At the university, Christian leaders studied Greek philosophy, and scholars like Celsus and Porphyry began to investigate the Christian Scriptures with a cool interest in this latest development of religious thought, critically pointing out the difficulties of the Old Testament and the inconsistencies of the New. By the beginning of the 3rd century, catechetical instruction in the churches

ON NURTURING CHRISTIANS

of Alexandria had developed into a regular school. Some of the students were converts preparing for baptism, some were Christians preparing for the priesthood, some were uncommitted seekers, and some were serious critics. Instruction was given at many levels in Hebrew and Christian scriptures, in the "preparatory studies" (geometry, arithmetic, and philosophical systems), and in "all branches of secular and philosophic learning." Clement, the first distinguished name of the faculty, is said to be "the father of Greek theology," tying Christianity to Hellenism and establishing Christianity as a philosophy. Origen, who followed him at Alexandria and perhaps surpassed him in scholarship, may be called "the first great dogmatist" of Christianity, and a 19th-century historian whose judgment is unassailable said that "orthodox theology has never yet advanced beyond the circle first mapped out by his mind."

After the fall of Rome and with the survival of the Dark Ages as the primary task, theology was fixed as formal and correct thinking about religion. For a millennium the church presented itself to mankind, in varying degrees of thoroughness, as the controller of human life, not only of acts but of thought. Theology became the struggle to maintain some arena of live action. It was found in the almost limitless capacity of the mind, aided by sophisticated tools of dialectic, to think about controlled issues in different ways and unexplored relationships. The one great threat to that control came in the proposal to substi-

NURTURING

tute Aristotelian logic for the Platonic thought on which Christian orthodoxy had been built since Clement and Origen. The threat boiled for a century but was cooled with the total Christianization of Aristotle by Thomas Aquinas in the 13th century. The result was a new burst of dialectic thought under official control.

For several decades the Reformation promised to change the medieval understanding of theology. Luther in particular seemed to be doing theology by thinking with his heart. "One thing only is needful to a good life and Christian liberty," he wrote in the vibrant year of 1520, "the Gospel of Christ." God's Word, as contained in the Scriptures, is all anyone needs for saving belief, and it is to be "grasped or nourished" not by logic or sacramental observances but by "faith alone." In faith "Christ and the soul are made one flesh." Acts of mercy and kindness will come as a result. Therefore, Christianity is a life devoted to Christ and neighbor, "to Christ by faith and to neighbor by love." But Luther was a schoolman, and when even faith threatened to get out of control among the Anabaptists and in the Peasants' Revolt, he retreated to the lessons of professional theology. With Melanchthon to aid, a system of schools was organized to reestablish thought about religion as the fortress of Reformation theology. "The truths of religion and moral duty," said Melanchthon, "cannot be rightly perceived except by minds soundly prepared by a training based upon the prac-

ON NURTURING CHRISTIANS

tice of past ages." Scholasticism became Protestant.

For the most part, teaching theology has continued to be "the right perception" of "minds soundly prepared." It has been an adult occupation and largely for clergymen. From time to time the forms of logic used for thinking about religion have changed: in the 18th century it was almost exclusively idealistic; in the 19th century it was largely scientific; in the 20th century it has been characteristically pragmatic. Toward the end of the 20th century, it is becoming technocratic. Rather consistently, however, theology has been an intellectual exercise, practiced by professionals, learned in exclusive graduate schools, taught by lecturing, and mastered by memorizing. Even so, after having passed through three years of specialized theological training, most pastors claim not to be theologians, turning their parishioners' questions aside or quoting aphorisms from theological books.

⚜

As a result of what theology has become, the offer to teach theology is seldom greeted with enthusiasm. Laymen tend to be suspicious of the subject.

The general impression is that theology is exotic and not for ordinary, street-corner people. It is thought to be carried on primarily in some foreign place like a dusty library deep in the heart of a vine-encrusted, gothic-windowed institution, and the uni-

NURTURING

versal visual image of *homo theologicus* is a dried-out creature blinking perennially and near-sightedly at the unaccustomed light of day. In the course of an ordinary conversation, ranging through a dozen usual subjects, in an airplane or bar with a chance acquaintance, one answers, "I'm a theologian." "Oh," comes the response with a cooling inflection, "you don't look like a theologian," and the instantly de-animated conversationalist drifts off to invest his time with a conventional mortal.

Theology is also thought to be esoteric. It is assumed that theology is conducted in language no one else understands because it depends heavily on Latin roots and consists of multisyllabled words. The theologian is expected often to say such words as "omniscient," "omnipresent," and "omnipotent," to say nothing of *"Stipendia enim peccati mors."* His subject matter is expected to be ancient events such as the Council of Nicaea, which, of course, is to be distinguished absolutely from the Council of Chalcedon to say nothing of Fourth Lateran and Vatican II. And he is expected to talk about God, whom no man hath seen and to most of whom he is an oblong blur at best. How does one carry on a conversation in a subject like that? Thus, when a theologian does chance to say something quite simple in single syllables, such as "God is love," to say nothing of "God is dead," the average layman says he finds the sentence unintelligible and turns to straightforward matters like the Dow Jones averages and the GNP.

ON NURTURING CHRISTIANS

Further, most laymen suppose that the only life-result of all these exotic and esoteric activities is controversy. People seem to argue most heatedly when religious beliefs are at stake, especially when they differ only slightly. Theology produces bad blood between brothers, and often enough in history, spilled blood: the Crusades, the Inquisition, the Thirty Years' War, the Salem Witch Trials, North and South Ireland, Fundamentalists and Modernists. Theology, much like the military, is for professionals, and most laymen don't want to be drafted.

⚜

Yet, one of the clear implications of the principle of "the priesthood of all believers" is that everyone shall be his own theologian. Perhaps the problem is that we seem to know only one understanding of theology—thinking about religion—and only one way to teach it—specialized unilateral instruction. The two associate naturally: both "thinking about" and "unilateral instruction" depend upon one-way communication between two points clearly removed from each other.

Still, religious experience has not died out, though from time to time it seems to have been on the wane, and now may be such a time. Therefore, thinking-with religion has been successfully communicated, and not, since it remains recognizably Christian even

NURTURING

in this time of rapid change, merely by the heretics as cynics suggest.

Jesus was a man who thought with his religious awareness, and it led him to take up a stance toward people, ideas, and governments. He was not a schoolman, but he taught. And people were moved in their hearts and found the experience shaping what they did and said. His teaching seems to have been a combination of saying, doing, and being. It occurred not in a classroom but in the course of daily events: walking, fishing, eating, resting, debating. Sometimes it happened more or less formally: people gathered and he spoke to them as they listened, but it probably little resembled address as we know it. There is no way to be certain, of course, for there were no tape recorders or movie cameras, but the sentence structure strongly suggests that he taught on these occasions as Eastern holy men still teach: a little story and a pause for reflection; a sentence or two, carefully polished through hours of meditation, and a pause. Though perhaps no one else spoke, the silences were filled with dialogue. On other occasions, conversation crackled into open challenge, and the repartee was unglossed and direct. For the rest, what was said was incidental to what was being done: people forgiven of guilt, relieved of disease, enlisted into loving. All this carried authenticity because the message was borne in the man himself: he was there with them, experiencing what they experienced,

ON NURTURING CHRISTIANS

thinking as he asked them to think, and in their presence developing the stance with people and toward history that brought him at last, in their full view, to death. Stance-taking in terms of religious experience was so effectively taught that the world was never the same again.

The model for theology is probably there rather than in the doctrines, and the model for teaching is probably there, too, rather than in the schools. Through the centuries, the mystics have taught that way, though their theology has seldom been able to stand the tests of analysis or orthodoxy. Through taking a stance toward everything based in all-consuming religious experience, they have tended to gather into communities separated from the world and characterized by special rules of life and conduct: the nurture of direct relationship to God was the only thing that mattered, and all else was to be minimized or excluded. There have been some notable examples: the brotherhood of preaching and serving that formed around Francis of Assisi before it was organized by the church into a safe and useful order; the Brethren of the Common Life in late medieval Holland, whose members took no lifelong vows and lived simply, earning their bread by teaching children and copying books, forming in time a theology of "imitating Christ" now associated with the name of Thomas a Kempis, and in turn influencing the German Reformation. In the 17th century, the Pietistic schools of August Hermann Francke,

NURTURING

in which it was assumed that the foundation of all learning was "true and pure love toward God and Man"; in spite of enormous difficulties they cared for thousands of children and influenced the emerging school systems of Germany. Johann Heinrich Pestalozzi's 18th-century orphanage schools conducted on a large farm with his wife Gertrude as mother; Pestalozzi called learning "organic"—an interrelation of "head, hand and heart"—and said that "life teaches," forbidding all textbooks: "This is not a school," exclaimed a visiting parent, "it is a family!" All these attempted, according to their own lights, to nurture a religious experience and to allow thinking to be formed by it.

⚜

Theological thinking is the act of taking a position in life in terms of religious experience. It is not thinking formed elsewhere in life, say by the sciences or analysis, applied to religion; it is rather thinking formed by religious experience applied to everything and anything in life, including science and analysis.

Religious experience, as reported in the Old and New Testaments as well as in numerous documents since then, seems to involve God and a person in relation to persons and the world. Often in experience the elements are paired off: person to persons, person to world, person to God, and so on through the possible doublets. In religious experience, however, all are related simultaneously. And, further, in such a way that the completeness and individuality of each is enhanced. The view that encompasses all that is sometimes called "wholeistic," and it seems to be characteristic of the Old Testament.

Judging from the way ancient Hebrews viewed the covenant and early Christians the incarnation, both are metaphors of the way God relates to man. The covenant was between Yahweh and his people and their leaders in relation to the Promised Land and for the sake of history and everyone outside the covenant. It was initiated and maintained by Yahweh, but it was never operative until the people accepted and acted on it, certifying its reciprocity. The incarnation was a gift by God for everyone who would see and believe, and each one who does accepts the burden of offering the invitation to others. It was "God in Christ, reconciling the world to himself," and in this instance "world" meant everything here, all nature and all time as well as all people. By reconciliation—the establishment of mutuality—every thing reaches its intended nature and the divine work of creation is continued to its completion.

So far as we can understand with our limited experience of personhood, at its completest there is no separation of activities. We think at one time, act at another, and feel at another, but with God "to be" is "to think, act and feel"—wholeistically. Thus, with considerable reservation, we may say that it would seem that the way God apparently relates to man in

NURTURING

the covenant and the incarnation is the way God "thinks." For us, theology should be God-thinking: seeing everything whole, relating that way, standing to life that way.

It is likely that this sort of standing-in-life is far more instinctive in childhood in our time than it is in adulthood. For somewhat more than two millennia we have been trained to think linearly: major premise, minor premise, conclusion, QED; problem, data, hypothesis, experiment, solution. Artists probably think more wholeistically than most people in our society. Creative thought, in science or business or politics or art, is probably wholeistic in nature.

It is the task of Christians to clarify the ground and enlarge the arena of thinking-with-religion. Christian nurture implies the theologizing of life. By definition the result appears to be the same as the process, and by example it appears to be caring, loving, suffering, serving, forgiving, creating, redeeming.

✣

Theology—taking the stance of thinking with one's religion about everything—is difficult to do well. Still, the subject is the most important and fragile on earth—and in the waters under the earth and in the heavens beyond the earth. The stance is built step-by-step, wholeistically. It is not so much an addition to nurturing as an interrelated element of it. Therefore, if Christian nurturing has been going on, the task is already being done. If the Bible is being taught-and-learned in accordance with its own nature, the source of theology is present. If the community of caring is being taught-and-learned, the scene is set and at work.

The task of helping children and young people to think relationally is not one that has been much considered. For the most part, the curriculum of the public schools and the method by which it is conducted and the system in which it is administered reinforce linear forms. Christian nurture is not without accomplices, however, in accomplishing its own agenda. Intuition is on our side: the first and instinctive response to real situations is almost always unified. So is the multilinear world of television: the mosaic of the picture-tube is more like Hebrew thought than Greek syllogisms. And so is the "new math": discoveries about the capacity of the first-grader to grasp set-theory have led to more wholeistic methods of beginning reading.

During the last two decades, Jean Piaget's theories of intellectual development have become enormously influential in American educational circles. Piaget is a French-writing Swiss psychologist of learning whose personal understanding of children and adolescents seems to be as significant to his theories as his more objective research. There are two basic principles, which have been observed already in these pages: conceptualizing is built on experiencing, and each subsequent level of capacity is built on all the pre-

NURTURING

ceding levels of achievement. Thinking appears to be fashioned from a sequence of sensation, perception, and finally the formation of concepts. Concepts tend to change with growing experience, becoming more numerous, complex, abstract. This sequence is found to occur in four more or less distinct stages. First is the *sensory motor level*, usually characterizing the first two years of life and defined by perceptive and motor functions in dealing with objects; language is used for retaining direct experience. Next comes the level of *preoperational* (or intuitive) thought, usually taking about five years, which is characteristically egocentric (internalized), single-focus (dealing with isolated features of the environment), and irreversible (because it works only in a forward logical direction from cause to effect). The third period is called *concrete-operational* thought, ordinarily in ages seven to eleven, and evidences both inductive and deductive logic but limited to concrete situations, visual and sensory data used directly and relied upon, and reversible logic (because it also works from consequences to effects), but little generalization. The fourth period is *formal-operational* (or abstract) thought and characterizes thinking from twelve onward; it is defined by the ability to think hypothetically, situations being seen in terms of propositions rather than of data and tested in thought rather than in actuality, and reasoning by inference and implication.

Ronald Goldman, a British psychologist, has adapted his notion of religious thinking to this conception and studied it in relation to Piaget's outline. For Piaget the ideal form of thought appears to be linear, and for Goldman religious thinking is linear thinking *about* religion. "Religious thinking," toward which childhood is making, is therefore impossible at the lowest stages. In the later stages, Goldman discovers from his research a "lag" in the development of "religious thinking": concrete thought, according to Piaget, begins at age seven, but in "religious thinking" not until eight, according to Goldman; "abstract thought" begins at about twelve, but in religion not until thirteen or fourteen.

This may be all the demonstration we need that linear thinking is not instinctive in the field of religion: children resist (or have a difficult time) applying it to religion because they sense the inappropriateness of reducing personal (multilinear) experience to nonpersonal (linear) forms. Linear thinking *is* an abstraction from life experiencing: "to abstract" is "to stand away" or "to stand off," to withdraw from the thing itself to view it as if it were separated from all else, including the observer. Linearity is a straight line drawn between only two of many possible points. It is a difficult lesson to learn, and this is, of course, the reason it comes so late in individual development and was not achieved by Western culture until the 19th century. It should be expected that children would take longer to learn to apply abstract thinking to religious experience

NURTURING

than to anything else. The task, therefore, in nurturing the Christian stance, is to establish multilinear, interrelational, personal thinking as the form of thinking most appropriate to religious experience.

The following suggestions are generalizations only. Each child will differ, and each group of learners will differ in capacity and pace. It must also be remembered that teaching-and-learning theology is only one part of Christian nurturing: it takes place in the context of nurturing the source and the scene, both of which are going on continuously.

⚜

AGES FOUR AND FIVE: *giving-and-receiving love.*

The actual exchange of love is the only safe bridge between abstract-thinking adults and preoperational-thinking children. From the beginning, children should hear the names of God and Jesus Christ on the lips of those who love God and Jesus and of those who love them as children. The essential elements of multilinear experience are thus present. However, it is easy for this practice to become saccharine rather than natural. The holy names should be pronounced as real names, which they are, of real beings, which they are. The fact that they are not visually present is likely to pose more difficulty for the teachers than for the children: children know a great deal about absentee loved ones, beginning with the disappearance of Mommy behind the apron playing peek-a-boo, and including grandparents who are no less real or loved because they live in Des Moines and are not visible. When the Old Testament stories use Hebrew names such as Yahweh or Elohim, let the children hear them: they need have no more trouble than with the fact that they have more than one name themselves. The colorful variety of activities ascribed to God in many of the biblical stories is instinctive in the child's thought-world and needs the simple reinforcement of acceptance by adults: he fights in battles, talks to his friends, rides the thunderclouds, is angry with disobedience, rewards goodness, loves his children whether or not they deserve it, plays in the oceans, creates the world. The mixture is difficult only for abstract thinkers. For preoperational thinkers it is proof of personal reality.

AGES SIX AND SEVEN: *encounter with significant people who care.*

Perhaps the most important theological experience at this age is enlarging the web of personal relationships toward the edge of the limited infinity of childhood comprehension. The personal world of the first- and second-grader is ordinarily bounded by home, school, and church. People float in and out of these worlds without concrete identification: visitors in the home, administrators and service people at the schools, functionaries at the church. When these people become real through personal contact, multi-

NURTURING

linearity is reinforced. Let them come into the religious classroom and establish their individuality in terms of who they are and what they do in the adult —"outside"—world, because they, too, care about children and pronounce the name of God as that of a friend. This relationship should be established in the context of class activities and in conversation. They should not come to give talks about themselves or present lectures about their vocations. Entering the child's world may take several hours, of course, but they need only be themselves: in being with the class a physician will do and say things that characterize him, and a janitor will be himself as fully and concretely. It is the genius of religion to deal with, not to talk about. Children instinctively know how.

AGES EIGHT TO TWELVE: *acquaintance with greatness.*

In this period when the child is learning to perform the first functions that Piaget can call thinking, i.e., concrete-operational, Christian nurture should enlarge the arena of multilinear thought and resist the linearization of thought in relation to religious experience.

Accordingly, *stretching* is the goal and method of nurturing. In the earlier years of this period, let the child's acquaintance be stretched from interesting local people to the most noble, exciting, daring, and loving people history can offer. His relation to them should be concrete: about that Piaget was right, and

ON NURTURING CHRISTIANS

religious thinking is no less concrete than formal thinking. Biography, personal writings and data, local color, historical settings—everything that will help them become real persons, though physically *in absentia,* to the learners.

The best teachers for this age are biographers: storytellers who care enough about their subjects to introduce them as friends, with real feeling for Paul's thorn-in-the-side, Luther's constipation, Jonathan Edwards' warts, Søren Kierkegaard's back; religious people who care about the inside of Augustine's experience in the garden, John's dark night of the soul, Judson's call to teach Christianity to the Orient.

In the later years of this period, let the child be stretched by personal acquaintance with great ideas. By setting ideas in the heads and lives of real persons, the teacher of religion can get a jump on the development of formal thought and at the same time reinforce the appropriate multilinearity of religious thought. There is no need at this level to develop the consistency or intricacies of theological systems. It is infinitely better to expose growing minds to a living mixture of possibilities pushed into expression by the individualities of religious experience. An idea or two per person, showing how the ideas summarize his own God-meeting, is functional for the 11- and 12-year-olds. They should be prevented from becoming aphorisms by relating them to the source of life. They will rather be concretions of experience.

NURTURING

Children can concretely understand "reverence for life" in terms of music, medicine, and Africa; they can make operational sense of "practicing the presence of God" in terms of a monastery kitchen. It is in their piling up that multilinearity is strengthened: layer on layer on layer, a riotous mixture of insights providing breadth and color.

AGES THIRTEEN TO FIFTEEN: *accumulation of theological elements.*

This is the period when Piaget says formal-operational thought begins and Goldman finds a two-year lag in the capacity to apply abstract thinking to religion. Horace Bushnell suggested that a different approach to religious thinking is needed. Despairing of the unchristian spirit engendered by the conflict of opposing creeds in 19th-century New England, each making its own absolute claims—Unitarian *versus* Trinitarian, primarily—he proposed that in view of the infinity of the nature of God the truth about him was not best found by selecting one creed and doing battle for it, but rather by piling as many as possible on top of one another so that in the multiplicity of their points of view some approximation of the full truth might be discovered. Because young teen-agers are beginning to be able to deal with first-step abstractions, let them accumulate definitions of words used in theological discourse; because they need to stretch their religious experience with multiplicity, let them accumulate as many

ON NURTURING CHRISTIANS

different sorts of definitions as possible and compare them. The words can range the theological possibilities from Atonement to *Weltanschauung*. The result may be a comparative glossary: it will not be regarded as decisive by orthodox (that is, linear) theologians, but there will be more in these collections that is true and real than in any one theological system. The process of assembling them will contribute to the developing capacity to do operational thinking and will be illustrative of the multilinearity of religious thinking.

The search for definitions will lead naturally to the use of words in sentences, that is, in actual creedal assertions. These may begin with such simple statements as "God is love," or "our Heavenly Father," or "the Father Almighty," or "perfect thought thinking about itself." Collections of these will lead to collections of creeds: Apostles' and Nicene, Augsburg and Westminster Confessions, Barmen Declaration. With some attention to the reinforcement of religious thinking as a valid form of logical expression for religious experience, teen-agers may have no logical block at all about the notion that Jesus Christ is simultaneously "wholly man" and "wholly God."

AGES SIXTEEN TO EIGHTEEN: *functionalizing of theological elements.*

This is a period not plotted by Piaget. In abstract thinking it is probably a period of enlarging con-

NURTURING

stantly the skills of applying linear forms to areas of data: the life and physical sciences, sociology and psychology, philosophy. It is important in this period to establish the distinction and maintain the relation of tension between religious thinking and thinking about religion.

Thinking about religion should be practiced vigorously but consciously as an abstraction: it is talking about real things but the talking is removed from the real things. The experience of talking may be concrete—and, for that matter, religious—but the subject is abstract. There should be debate about religious propositions—themselves an abstraction. It should be led by adults practiced in insisting on rigor, quick to spy fallacies in formal linear logic, and ingenious at exposing them. The leaders should be knowledgeable about the data of the sources and scenes of religious experience, so that they can authoritatively recall wide-ranging adolescent discussions to the factual data. Above all, they must be adults capable of keeping the discussion, for all its rigor, in the arena of love. This is apt to be more difficult for them than for the teen-agers. Adults with these qualities are difficult to find; they are likely to be either under thirty or over sixty, to think more than they talk, and to have seen a great deal of life.

Thinking with religion, however, is the primary task. Fired with the discovery of abstract thinking, adolescents need to be reminded constantly that the world of concrete data is neither linear nor simple, and that formal logic is always in danger of becoming too far removed from the data themselves. They need to be exposed continually to some adult leaders who are capable of recalling them from flights of intellectual fancy to the specific world of religious relationships. These adults will constantly be reminding their learners that religious concepts occur in sets, and leading them in the exercise of that sort of logic. Death will surely come in for discussion by adolescents: leaders will be people who can conduct the discussion of death in terms of a set of concept-experiences such as life-joy-sadness-birth and the like, who can insist that the discussion of God be in a set-group such as man-comraderie-suffering-creating-celebration and the like, and incarnation in terms of Nazareth-carpentry-nationalism-sin-forgiveness-crucifixion-resurrection and the like. It is no accident that the religion which occurs only in community can be talked about appropriately only in terms of a community of ideas.

ADULTHOOD: *refinement*.

Thinking never stops until life does. The difficulty is that in a technological society the pressure of daily events and ordinary thought is to secularize religious thinking. The need to simplify everything into workable solutions for daily and ever-ready problems needs to be countered by the recovery of origins: the origins of religious experience and wholeistic thinking. Adulthood is an opportunity to apply the

NURTURING

religious way of thinking to everything as life brings it up for consideration. Adults need support in that. One source is the more natively multilinear thinking of children. Another, discovered by many adults accidentally, is the arts.

⚜

Throughout the process of nurturing religious thinking, two methods are constantly available and should be practiced: opportunities for renewed religious experience and for trans-verbal expression of it.

The religious stance toward everything is nurtured by specific religious experiences. There will be special occasions of all sorts: worship events, festivals, celebrations, shared meals, retreats, meditation—alone, in the presence of others, in nature. One of the essential dimensions of theological thinking is time; one of the essential motifs is withdrawal-and-return.

Everyone should be given every possible opportunity and support for expressing religious thinking nonverbally: music, painting, dance, drama; banners, posters, celebrations. The linear forms of grammar need to be experimented with as the conscious saying of things first explored and said less verbally. "Poets," Horace Bushnell once exclaimed, "are the best metaphysicians." There must also be instruction in the grammar of all these forms of expression so that the media are a release rather than a frustration.

ON NURTURING CHRISTIANS

And time to try: alone, in the presence of others, in nature. One of the essential dimensions of theological expression is practice; one of the essential motifs, creating-and-sharing.

⚜

Christian nurturing implies the discovery of forms of thought and expression appropriate to religious experience, and the relating of religious thinking to everything. It is something of a frontier in contemporary education.

4. Style

In nurturing Christians, style is the result of giving-and-receiving the source, the scene, and a stance. Teaching and learning style is the action of integrating and creating mutually.

The early Christians would have said "following The Way." Paul wrote to Corinth of "the highest way of all," characterized by faith, hope, and love. To Galatia he wrote of the fruits of the Spirit in human living: love, joy, peace, patience, kindness, generosity, fidelity, adaptability, and self-control. To Ephesus he wrote of taking a stand in life equipped with truth, righteousness, peace, salvation, the Word, faith. Today, social scientists might prefer to speak

ON NURTURING CHRISTIANS

of "developing a life-style." What is meant is putting it all—history, community, and theology—together in such a fashion that something more than the sum of the parts results in the lives of both learners and teachers.

In any case, wholeness is what Christian nurturing is all about, all the time, all the way.

⚜

The drive for unity is one of the most powerful in human experience. It is something like an insistent itch at the unreachable bottom of our hearts. It will not let us alone. It spurs us on like hunger or a tormenting question. Since psychology has come of scientific age, one dare not speak of instinct, but the urge to wholeness might be called an impulse as primitive as the urges for food, rest, and sex.

The opposite is a sense of disjointedness in things, and that may be one of the most persistent problems of current times. "A severed hand is an ugly thing," wrote Robinson Jeffers from his cliff above Carmel Bay; "and man dissevered from the earth and stars and his history, for contemplation or in fact, often appears atrociously ugly."

Growing human disjointedness is one of the most common characteristics of the late 20th century. Never quite touching, never really seeing a face, we neither hate nor love, as Erich Fromm has noted: behind the formal front of friendliness there is only

NURTURING

distance, indifference, subtle mistrust. Life chatters on in half-awake lecture-halls, and one-way talk is assumed to be education. Tennessee Williams, in the preface to *Cat on a Hot Tin Roof*, speaks of "a lonely condition so terrifying to think about that we usually don't."

This kind of isolation has expressed itself politically through hypernationalism, intellectually through the proliferation of departments on campus and specializations in the world, economically through powerful corporations on the one side and powerful unions on the other, religiously through the multiplication of sects. As Camus says in *The Fall*, "For anyone who is alone, without God and without a master, the weight of days is dreadful."

We counter impulsively by yearning for connectedness. Jeffers continued: "The greatest beauty is / organic wholeness, the wholeness of life and things, the divine beauty / of the universe." The Apostle Paul wrote to the church at Corinth about the organic wholeness of love: "Our knowledge and our foresight are alike partial, and the partial vanishes when wholeness comes." Dante spoke of "the love which moves the sun and all the stars." A later poet was aware that he could not pick a wild flower without disturbing the stars. The drive to unite the discordant elements of the discomforting chaos with which we are confronted is unlimited. It may said to be open-ended.

ON NURTURING CHRISTIANS

✣

Thirty years ago, Lewis J. Sherrill, so far the last of perhaps a half-dozen "deans" of the Christian Education Movement in the United States, was using the word "wholth." It is a complicated and somewhat intricate pun.

Wholth includes the meaning of the word "whole," which in the Old Testament means "unseparated" or "united." Hebrew thought is "wholeistic" or "holistic" throughout, resisting everywhere the separation of things: body/mind, person/people, Yahweh/Israel. "Holy," in both Old and New Testaments, means "united": holiness is the state of being whole, that is, unified in oneself and in one's relation to persons, the world, and God. In philosophy, "wholeness" refers to The Totality, The Absolute, The Macrocosm: that entity which is greater than the sum of its parts. The relation of parts to wholes has fascinated philosophers in all ages.

Wholth includes the meaning of the common word "health." We know it as a medical term. In the psychological and biological senses it is used when all parts of an organism are functioning appropriately so that its goals may be achieved. It is defined by illness. Illness is a specific malfunction which may be identified and the causes determined. Health is an absence of illness but is itself not so easily described as the negative condition.

Wholth means to include the meaning of the

NURTURING

word "worth." What Sherrill had in mind was "basic human worthfulness" and the creative psychological result of sensing one's own worth. Human worthfulness is the cornerstone of democracy: like health, it is best known by its absence, those circumstances in which a democratic society denies it to some of its citizens. In a totalitarian society the absence is hardly noted. Worthfulness is also the foundation of ethics: the Golden Rule is often cited as a standard of action taking worth seriously, both in oneself and in others. Worthfulness is a theological principle: a human being claims worth because he is loved by God. It has been pointed out that worth is one of the root words of worship (worth-ship), which may be defined as the act of ascribing supreme worth to God.

And finally, wholth—in the context of Christian nurturing—has the advantage of sounding as if it might have been used by the King James translators of the Bible.

⚜

Christian nurturing seeks the style of wholth in life as a way of life: it is the process of laying parts into life so that life may be whole.

The teacher is a person who sees the vision of wholeness. He makes no pretense of having achieved it, but he acknowledges that the vision exposes him to the reality of it and the potentiality of achieving it. His is a fascination with the possible impossibility.

ON NURTURING CHRISTIANS

So he concerns himself with experiencing the source of religion, joining the religious scene, and building a religious stance in life. His experience shows him that each ends in mystery: the love of God, the trans-human *agape* love. Having seen the vision, he is interested in knowing how wholeness looks and feels from the learner's side of experience. He accepts the privilege of moving with the learners to the far edge of experience where they, too, find the mystery of divine love awaiting them.

The learner is a person seeking wholeness. Persons are constantly changing beings. They are driven by experience, that continuous interaction between the objective, out-side world of personal beings and physical things, and the subjective, in-side world of selfhood. Both the interchange and the elements are in constant flux. Especially in childhood and adolescence, but also throughout adulthood, persons' bodies are changing. The period of childhood physical growth comprises "the wonder years," as a food advertisement has it: the sheer pressure of physical enlargement forces an acute awareness of parts and wholes. It is surpassed, however, by the biological changes of adolescence as a source of personal change and an awareness of wholth. The process of biological change continues, less spectacularly, throughout life. Intellectual capacity is also in constant change: through memory, the accumulation of observation and association, thinking changes. These complex and constant changes expose persons, will-they/nill-

NURTURING

they, to the capacity for wholeness: the appropriate interrelation of parts into functioning unity. We are all, in short, learners always, all ways.

Together—and now the preposition assumes full significance—teacher and learners as persons seeing and seeking the possibility of wholeness come to the edge of the mystery. Seeking a unity of parts they have probed together into a new dimension, and the act breaks through into new life. Paul called it "the New Being."

A quest for wholth is the Christian life-style.

✣

Life-style is a womb-to-tomb, life-wide matter. It is a unity forged of the materials of growth in the fires of change.

Infancy is a period of unmeasurable growth. Relatively, more growth takes place during infancy than in any other period of life: from nothingness to readiness for life in three years! Probably the biological development is most important as well as most observable. Physical growing and skill mastery are the consuming tasks, and they require enormous amounts of fuel, practice, and support. Still, Freud once observed that the child had a philosophy of life by the time he was five, Adler said it was established by the end of the first year, and Jung was so impressed by it that he could only account for it by reference to a racial history bequeathed to the child entire. In

ON NURTURING CHRISTIANS

any event, all this appears to be development achieved by a human being at the mercy of other persons, chiefly, of course, in the home. Here he has the advantage of being managed by persons who love him, or who are at least tied to him by dependency and constant association.

Childhood is a period devoted largely to social growth. Physical growth continues but levels off in the later years. The primary task of childhood is becoming an individual. This discovery is largely directed by other persons. The school takes over much of the task of directing growth and though peer-groups become more and more important, child life is still dominated by adults.

Adolescence is a period dominated by psychological tasks. It is a conscious adventure into as yet unknown worlds. The chief undertaking is attempting to find a balance of forces for himself—between male and female, reason and emotion, patience and impatience, authority and freedom. It is a period of wanting to do everything for himself but learning that home and society are not yet ready to give him the chance unless he either demands it or earns it.

Young adulthood is a period of challenges. The young adult is faced with a sequence of decisions that sometimes seems to be never-ending: military service, political partisanship, religion, vocation, location, marriage, family. They are decisions for which he is held responsible. Yet it often seems that he has been given little preparation for decision-making.

NURTURING

Much of his time and energy are spent in making choices and living with the results. He is often exhausted, sometimes over-challenged.

Middle adulthood is a period of achievement. The decisions he made as a young adult now begin to show for all to see in his possessions, income, status. He must begin to settle scores with his dreams. The search is for some sort of satisfaction. In the effort to be satisfied with his early decisions, he tends to let old judgments decide new problems. Or he may find nothing satisfactory and keep young adulthood alive by continuing to make new decisions or finding new challenges to meet.

Late adulthood is a period of simplification. The predominance of the quest for results passes away. Possessions, income, and status diminish in importance. Habit is substituted for decision-making, and adventure is less attractive. There is time for thought and memory.

The style characterizing a life grows out of these materials and changes.

♣

At each stage, in each change, one is exposed to the reality of God. People, however, respond differently.

THE ROMANTIC STYLE: *responding to life by finding God comforting.* The style is to shrink: life is regarded as a problem to be dealt with as safely as possible.

In infancy the child may simply not identify God. In the view that God is real, this is an evasion. It may occur because he has been over-loved and given too much parental, or substitute-parental, protection from growth. He may attempt to evade God if God has been too much talked-about in adult terms which have no meaning, or the wrong meaning, for him. Non-identification need not be verbalized, of course, to be real, and comes into full view only later.

The child tends to relate to God in terms of his own individual sense of belonging, which is becoming established through the social pressures of life. If he finds God a threat to his developing individuality, he tends to withdraw into the indeterminate and unchallenging we-identifications of his infancy. Ordinarily, however, toward the end of childhood he finds a comfortable relation to God in terms of his social relationships.

The adolescent is interested in how God figures in the adventures of youth. If he finds God to be too much a strain on his intelligence and always propelling him into unprepared experiences of love and trust, he may withdraw into the comfortable feelings of childhood. Jesus, the happy boy of Nazareth, the gentle and smiling encourager of the poor and depressed, the man who proposed that everybody treat others as he would wish to be treated, the simple idealist, may become the focus of a cultism.

NURTURING

The young adult who is over-challenged may tend to postpone solving problems. He may not get married, and if he does he may not have children; he may move about among jobs; and he may evade making any commitments to a distinctive life-style. His retreat may well be into the individualism and adventurism of youth, but he is more likely to leapfrog into the security of childhood.

The middle adult may become cautious in the ways he does everything, conservative in his political and social positions. He tends to lean on the Bible literally and simply interpreted as an ancient (or "timeless") document. He may keep up a minimal church identification. He prefers that the church be an institution, well-organized, well-run, and well-mannered. God is understood to be the upholder of the *status quo*.

The late adult finds in God his eternal support. Change and decay in all around he sees, but God is the one who changes not, a Rock of Ages. The chief function of deity is to support the afterlife of human beings. He tends to become physically dependent and psychologically helpless long before there is biological need to do so.

In the romantic religious style, God is real enough at every stage: he is the God of the monks and saints and other otherworldly sorts.

THE HEROIC STYLE: *responding to life by finding God exciting*. The style is to plunge: life is

ON NURTURING CHRISTIANS

regarded as a series of events to be conquered, problems to be beaten.

The infant may have felt unloved. He tends to resent the loving God adults spend so much time talking about. The resentment may become overt later, now it may show only as attempting to dominate other children in class and play, especially in the church school classroom which is identified especially with love-and-God.

The child is finding most satisfaction in the task of self-identification by focusing on otherness. He is abrasive in his personal relationships, perhaps. Perhaps he substitutes objects for people, becoming interested in mechanics of one sort or another, and spends his time engineering things. Perhaps he treats people as objects, spending his time engineering them. His religious experience may be more or less naturalistic, mystic experiences outdoors which demonstrate the otherness, majesty, and objectivity of God.

The adolescent may find that the turmoil of his period and among his peers is all to his liking. By resisting authority or trends he can add to the chaos he enjoys. Especially if his peers are interested in religious experience, he may take up an atheistic or agnostic stance. He makes alarms so that he can observe other people coping with them. Or so that he may cope with them himself. Religion is the support of reform and God the great iconoclast.

The young adult may begin the role of conquerer.

NURTURING

He overpowers opposing athletes, competitors for advancement, institutions, problems. He overcomes persons intellectually, socially, and sexually. He may deny the existence of God as a way of overcoming him. Or he may feel that God supports him, or has even called him, personally in conquering others.

The middle adult may now feel that God is definitely on his side, if not personally, then ideologically or at least socially, racially, nationally. He is therefore self-assured. If he is a churchman, he is interested in the quantitative and competitive aspects of his church: membership, budget, buildings. All always increasing, of course. If he does not succeed in his own projects, he may find ways to rationalize God's lack of support, such as other people's sinfulness or lack of intelligence.

The late adult is often somewhat sad, a little frightened by his life story as he begins to recall and recount it. Failing physical powers may prevent him from eternally overcoming everything, and he may recover his adolescent religion of otherness.

In the heroic style, God is real enough at every stage: he is the God of the imperialists, world-conquerers, and crusaders.

THE WHOLEISTIC STYLE: *responding to life by finding God creating*. The style is to transform: what may be called creativity in God and transformation in humans turns out to be the mutually achieved divine-human action of making what was partial whole.

The Romantic Style is essentially a childhood style. It is completely appropriate to childhood. There is therefore an authenticity about it which haunts the rest of life. Many developmental psychologists have noted the plateau that often occurs at the peak of childhood. The biological growing tasks of childhood have been completed and everything seems to be in balance and the child is physically coordinated to a remarkable degree. He understands the limited world he experiences, and moves through it with great poise. There is winsome charm in this innocent childlikeness. It is often the happiest time of an individual's life. It is a precarious plateau, however. The earthquakes of adolescence are about to strike. The world can never be the same again. The memory of the childhood plateau is therefore often saturated with nostalgia. But it no longer exists, and to try to find it again or to live later as if it still existed, is childishness. Retreating may be sweet, but it is also bitter. There is an inescapable partiality that defeats maturity.

The Heroic Style is essentially an adolescent style. It is appropriate to adolescence. There is often a much smaller plateau in the late teen years or early years of the twenties. Frequently it comes in college, often in the senior year. The life of intellectual and social adventure is continuously exciting. Competition is productive. The tools of intellectual inquiry

NURTURING

have been mastered and may be used with precision and certainty. The techniques of campus fun-life produce many pleasures. There is something enormously gratifying about the unity of energy and capacity, place and performance. Some, often the most successful, choose to stay on in college: graduate work, teaching, administration. Some may carry the adolescent spirit out into the world, which becomes for them a limitless campus to be lived in and conquered in adolescent style. Of course, the high plateau may be reached off campus and by those who have never lived there. There is, however, something fundamentally tragic about life when the eternal adolescent loses excitement and energy. Life cannot be a continuous dinner party at which all the guests are twenty years old.

Both styles are authentic, but both are partial. The question for nurturing, therefore, is how a whole-response may be nurtured.

One part of the answer is that *the* Christian style is never fixed and complete. Life is an interrelated series of events each of which may be made whole; the nature of the sum total does not yet appear but can be trusted. In spite of immediate anxieties and insecurities, growth continues in hope and trust. The style-of-life is, precisely, a questing style.

Another part of the answer is that wholeness is comprised of parts. The tendency to shrink back and the challenge to conquer are each momentarily adequate but even then are in passage into a level at which they are inadequate. Each exposes the person at its moment of reality to God. Each closes its revelational possibilities when its appropriate moment has passed. Those experiences of passage should in themselves be justification of faith in the next steps.

These and other parts of an answer suggest the whole answer to the question of nurturing: *wholth becomes the style of the entire process and of each moment in it.*

Nurturing Christians is no more or less than a series of shared moments to be made whole by the presence and love of God.

It is now possible to speak of "disappearing teachership." The teacher joins the learners in the attempt to turn life into a pilgrimage. The teacher crosses over to the learner's side of experience, and together they face God in life. With teachers and learners standing on the learning side of experience, the role of teaching is given to God. He teaches life.

⚜

There are two spin-offs at each point in the nurturing process, and each serves the other. They are not educative strategies but signs that education is occurring.

Activity on behalf of others. Christian nurturing will always produce empathy for the human condition. In ages four and five and ages six and seven, the

NURTURING

task will be to know and be present to one another. During ages eight to twelve, the task will be helping one another among themselves, in the classroom and at home. During ages thirteen to fifteen, the enthusiasm for sharing often takes over. This may, indeed, be the most effective evangelistic group the Christian Movement has at its service. If there is doubt concerning the evangelicalism of the young teen-ager, consider the continuing history of teen-age fads and the recent history of the drug scene. During the succeeding period, ages sixteen to eighteen, the sharing is usually more oriented to action. It is the project-and-protest period. In adulthood, activity for others becomes ministry. A total lay ministry of the nurturing to the rest of the world should be expected. It has long been so. The 19th century alone saw prison reform, temperance, labor, youth, and welfare movements born in the church and given to the world for secularizing. In more recent times, women's rights, political action, racial integration, and peace have been spin-offs. Now may be the time for the nurturing Christian Movement to reform the schools.

Activity on behalf of God. Christian nurturing will always produce empathy for the divine-human condition. Where the quest is consciously for religious experience, moments of wholth will occur. They may come in elation, failure, discouragement, satisfaction. They are the times when event becomes transparent to depth and one can see into the deep sea bed of experience. It is the responsibility of the teacher to be alert for them. She will train herself to recognize, in the group of her learners, the signs of the time. And she will be ready to interrupt the educational process to mark the product. Worship is the celebration of wholth in its presence: the movement of time is held temporarily so that the dimension of infinity may be savored. Worship naturally takes place at the instant: eleven o'clock Sunday morning and the children's chapel down the hall are both sophisticated and often not very functional abstractions. Each event of worship will have its own character and leave behind its own residue. Each class will create and collect its mementoes and they will become the materials of other worship occasions: liturgies, songs, prayers, dances, artifacts.

⚜

Causes related to results are the trademark of Christian nurturing. Source, scene, and stance are component parts of the new and emerging whole that may be called the nurturing style.

⚜

In clarifying and actualizing religious experiencing, the Christian educator has his own thing to do.

If it is done well, it may not be popular in the church headquarters and it may be that the churches will not be enthusiastic about it. It is very different

NURTURING

from most of what is now called Christian education. It could stir things up considerably.

There is the chance that if the Christian nurturer can only say well what it is that he is trying to do well the public school educators may find in it the help they need.

EPILOGUE ✦ ✦

The Crusades were in many ways the most remarkable phenomenon of the early Middle Ages.

No enterprise of the dawning golden age of Western Europe better illustrates both the papal power and the medieval mind. "God, God, God," exclaimed a theologian, "nothing but God!" Everything reinforced that exclamation.

In the seventy years between 970 and 1040 there were forty-eight famine years. Then followed sickness and plague; the in-

ON NURTURING CHRISTIANS

vasions of the dreaded Turks, as medieval men called all the Moslems; baronial wars ravaging the harvests when there was a yield. Society was organized so that those at the top, those nearest God, received the best Europe had to offer, in times of shortages draining off from the bottom much of what was left to sustain life.

The result was a deepening of religious feeling. Monasticism and mysticism flourished. Miracles, demonstrating the possibility of escape from the expected and ordinary, became the talk of Europe, and it became popular to believe that one could secure some special advantages in the afterlife by visiting the scenes of miracles. In the south, there were some successful contests with the Mohammedans. Knighthood came to flower, and armored men on horseback began to share the widening paths of Europe with grubby pilgrims. There was everywhere an apocalyptic sense of impending change, and everybody seemed to sense that it would be religious in nature.

It was at this moment that Peter the Hermit rode across northern France, barefooted and bareheaded, carrying a huge wooden cross, preaching with fiery indignation the desecrations of the Infidel in the Holy Land. All Christendom stirred. Knights and laborers enlisted, also women,

EPILOGUE

children, old men, thieves, and prostitutes, and in time they all stirred about the holy places of Italy and Greece, anxious to ensure their souls against the torments of the hereafter. In 1096 a vast and motley crowd set out for the Holy Land itself on the First Crusade. They were massacred by the people whose land they crossed, defeated in Asia Minor by the Turks. Peter escaped, some legends say in a rearward direction, and at last caught up with a more disciplined military band, entering Jerusalem in 1099

Others followed for a century. Their names and stories are still widely known: Frederick Barbarossa, the greatest soldier of his century; Richard the Lion-Hearted, who spent two decades in Moslem prisons; Philip Augustus of France, a saintly soldier. Quarrels, booty, a stream of relics from ancient places to adorn European churches. No permanent conquest of the Holy Land, enormous cost in life and treasure. From it all the unintended and unforeseen change from the Dark Ages to the golden ones.

In the year 1212, a twelve-year-old shepherd boy, called Stephen, from the little town of Cloyes near Orleans, went to King Philip of France with a letter which he said came from Christ himself, bidding Stephen to organize a Crusade. In spite of

ON NURTURING CHRISTIANS

the King's disapproval, this strange shepherd boy announced that he would lead a crusade of children to rescue Christendom. He said that the sea would dry up before them to let them walk in safety to the Holy Land.

Such was his confidence and enthusiasm that children from many parts of France flocked to join him, and in June 30,000 young crusaders gathered for the great adventure. Most of them on foot and finding food and shelter where they could, they marched through central France and the hot dry summer to Marseilles.

In Germany, a boy of Cologne named Nicholas, son of a minor nobleman, gathered 20,000 children. They followed the path of the northern Crusaders, up the Rhine and across the Alps, where the unusually hot summer was in their favor. On the southern slopes they divided, and one group passed through Rome where they received the Pope's reluctant blessing and pressed on to Naples where they expected to find ships waiting. The other group worked their way down the eastern coast to Brindisi.

"A study in pathology," says one scholar. "A melancholy episode," says another. At the time, civil authorities scolded them for insolence. Churchmen accused

EPILOGUE

them of both blasphemy and heresy. They were only imitating what their elders had been doing for a century and putting into action the ideals of Christian heroism and nobility they had been taught since they could remember.

Stephen led his children into Marseilles and to the edge of the Mediterranean, but the sea did not dry up to let them walk as he had promised to the Holy Land. Then, miraculously and in what seemed to be the nick of time, two merchants appeared and offered to transport them, free of charge, to Palestine in their fleet of seven ships. Three days out they ran into storms, and two of the ships were wrecked. The rest reached the north coast of Africa where the children were sold into slavery. Some became interpreters and secretaries, others were put to death for refusing to become Moslems. Of all the children who started from France, only one ever returned.

The Crusade of German children disappeared into the Italian countryside. Only a few stragglers made their way back to Germany to participate in the golden age of medieval splendor made possible by the failure of the adult crusades of the century before.

ON NURTURING CHRISTIANS

Seven hundred and fifty years later a second children's crusade is gathering. Its goal, also, is salvation. Its Holy Land, however, is the School. And adults are much wiser now than they were.

BIBLIOGRAPHY ✣ ✣

Bailey, Albert E. *Daily Life in Bible Times.* New York: Scribner's, 1943.
Barrett, William. *Irrational Man.* Garden City, N.Y.: Doubleday, 1958.
Buber, Martin. *Between Man and Man.* Boston: Beacon Press, 1955.
———. *I and Thou.* New York: Scribner's, 1958.
———. *The Prophetic Faith.* Gloucester, Mass.: Peter Smith, 1949.
Bushnell, Horace. *Christian Nurture.* New York: Scribner's, 1860; New Haven: Yale University Press, 1966.
Carpenter, Joseph Estlin. *Life in Palestine.* London: The Lindsey Press, 1935.
Chase, Mary Ellen. *Life and Language in the Old Testament.* New York: W. W. Norton, 1955.

Coe, George Albert. *The Social Theory of Religious Education*. New York: Scribner's, 1917.

Dennison, George. *The Lives of Children*. New York: Random House, 1969.

Dewey, John. *The Child and the Curriculum*. Chicago: The University of Chicago Press, 1902.

———. *My Pedagogic Creed*. New York: E. E. Kellogg, 1897.

———. *The School and Society*. Chicago: The University of Chicago Press, 1915.

Ellul, Jacques. *The Technological Society*. New York: Knopf, 1964.

Erikson, Erik. *Childhood and Society*. New York: W. W. Norton, 1963.

Friedenberg, Edgar. *Coming of Age in America*. New York: Random House, 1965.

Fromm, Erich. *The Art of Loving*. New York: Harper, 1956.

Goldman, Ronald. *Religious Thinking—from Childhood to Adolescence*. London: Routledge-Kegan Paul, 1964.

Goodman, Paul. *Growing Up Absurd*. New York: Random House, 1960.

Heidegger, Martin. *Being and Time*. New York: Harper, 1962.

Henry, Jules. *Culture Against Man*. New York: Random House, 1963.

Herndon, James. *The Way It Spozed To Be*. New York: Simon & Schuster, 1968.

Holt, John. *How Children Fail*. New York: Pitman, 1964.

Illich, Ivan. *Deschooling Society*. New York: Harper, 1971.

Johnson, Aubrey. *The Vitality of the Individual in the Thought of Ancient Israel*. Cardiff: University of Wales, 1964.

BIBLIOGRAPHY

Jung, Carl. *Modern Man in Search of a Soul.* New York: Harcourt, Brace & World, 1933.

Keniston, Kenneth. *The Uncommitted.* New York: Harcourt, Brace & World, 1965.

Kohl, Herbert. *Open Classroom.* New York: Vintage Books, 1970.

―――. *36 Children.* New York: New American Library, 1967.

Kozol, Jonathan. *Death at an Early Age.* Boston: Houghton Mifflin, 1967.

Krishnamurti. *Education and the Significance of Life.* New York: Harper, 1953.

Laing, R. D. *The Politics of Experience and the Bird of Paradise.* London: Penguin, 1967.

Lau Tzu. *Tau Teh King.* Kerchonkson, New York: Poets Press, 1966.

Leonard, George. *Education and Ecstasy.* New York: Delacorte Press, 1968.

McLuhan, Marshall. *Understanding Media.* New York: McGraw-Hill, 1964.

Marcuse, Herbert. *One Dimensional Man.* Boston: Beacon Press, 1964.

May, Rollo. *Existential Psychology.* New York: Basic Books, 1958.

Maslow, Abraham. *Toward a Psychology of Being.* Princeton, N.J.: Van Nostrand, 1968.

Mumford, Lewis. *The Transformations of Man.* New York: Collier, 1956.

Neill, A. S. *Summerhill.* New York: Hart, 1960.

Piaget, Jean. *The Moral Judgment of the Child.* London: Routledge & Kegan Paul, 1932.

――― and Inhelder, Barbel. *The Psychology of the Child.* New York: Basic Books, 1969.

Polanyi, Michael. *Personal Knowledge.* Chicago: The University of Chicago Press, 1959.

Postman, Neil, and Weingartner, Charles. *The Soft Revolution*. New York: Dell Books, 1971.
Reich, Charles. *The Greening of America*. New York: Random House, 1970.
Richardson, Elwyn. *In The Early World*. New York: Pantheon Books, 1964.
Rogers, Carl. *The Freedom to Learn*. Columbus, Ohio: C. E. Merrill, 1969.
Rood, Wayne R. *The Art of Teaching Christianity*. Nashville: Abingdon Press, 1968.
―――. *Understanding Christian Education*. Nashville: Abingdon Press, 1970.
Roszak, Theodore. *The Making of a Counter Culture*. Garden City, N.Y., Doubleday, 1969.
Sherrill, Lewis J. *The Gift of Power*. New York: Macmillan, 1955.
―――. *The Struggle of the Soul*. New York: Macmillan, 1951.
Theobald, Robert. *An Alternative Future for America II*. 2nd. ed. Chicago: Swallow Press, 1970.
Thoreau, Henry D. *Walden*. Boston, 1854. New York: Modern Library, 1965.
Wright, G. E. *God Who Acts*. London: SCM Press, 1952.
―――. *The Biblical Doctrine of Man in Society*. London: SCM Press, 1950.